Castle Walks in Yorkshire

Castle Walks in Yorkshire

Peter R. Williamson

For Debbie ...

frontispiece: Castle Bolton.

First published in 2006
by Palatine Books,
Carnegie House,
Chatsworth Road
Lancaster LA1 4SL
www.palatinebooks.com

Copyright © Peter R. Williamson, 2006

All photographs are by P. R. Williamson, except frontispiece and page ix,
which are by the publisher

British Library Cataloguing-in-Publication data
A catalogue record for this book is available from the British Library

ISBN 10: 1-874181-32-3
ISBN 13: 978-1-874181-32-3

Typeset by Carnegie Book Production
www.carnegiebookproduction.com
Printed and bound in the UK by Cambridge University Press

Contents

Acknowledgements

There are many people who have helped with this book. At the fore
are those stalwart companions who have accompanied me through
hail, rain and sunshine on my quest to visit these castles. In particular,
heartfelt thanks to Debbie Jackson for her delightful company and for
her support, patience and encouragement. Also, for having to put up
with visiting yet more 'earthworks, banks and ditches' in my quest to
visit all the castle sites in Yorkshire.

I would also like to thank my parents for their help in researching
certain details. My father was invaluable in trawling through Pevsner
and many other learned tomes to glean information on the many
churches and monasteries that I passed, whilst my mother helped with
the identification of trees and plants.

There are other people from professional bodies who have helped
with information relating to the sites and access along certain routes.
They include Tracey Booth of Hull Local History Library; Nick
Boldrini, SMR Computing Officer, Heritage Unit at North Yorkshire
County Council; Kath Keith, West Yorkshire Archaeology Service,
Registry of Deeds in Wakefield; and Janet Mackley of The Moors
Centre at Danby. Plus, my thanks to local historians, John Goodchild
(Wakefield) and John Sheehan (Northallerton) for their help, and to
the nice people at Skipton Castle, who let me sneak in to take a few
photos from within the courtyard – as long as I didn't tell anybody!

Special thanks to Christopher Ussher and Laxmi Bhakta Bantawa MBE of the Harewood Estate for inviting me to visit and photograph Harewood Castle.

Thanks to Ivan Moorhouse, Tracey Flower and Gill Haynes for accompanying me on several of the walks and helping with route finding.

I would also like to thank some of the interesting people whom I met along the way, in particular, Mrs Kirk of Harlsey Castle and Mr Chapman from Paull Holme; whilst in Paull, Bob, who lives at No. 3 The Old Coastguard Cottages, invited me onto the roof of his house to get an unusual shot of Paull lighthouse with Hull docks beyond. Cheers, Bob!

Finally, thanks to Alistair and Anna and the team at Carnegie Publishing for allowing me the opportunity to research and write this book, thus fulfilling a long-held ambition.

Author's Note

I have long had two overriding passions: walking and visiting castles. This book aims to combine the two by directing walkers not only to some of the finest and most unusual castles in Yorkshire, but also to some lesser well-known sites.

There simply is not room in this book to include walks that visit all the castles in Yorkshire, and so I have had to be selective. Some are amongst Yorkshire's most popular visitor attractions. They still stand high and proud and give a detailed insight into life in the Middle Ages. Others are mere mounds of earth indicating where castles once stood. However, all are of equal importance and interest. All have a history and all have a place in this book.

The choice has been somewhat dictated by geographic location as I wished to cover the whole county as much as possible. Therefore, some celebrated castles, like Pontefract and Richmond, have been omitted in favour of less well-known sites, like Burstwick, Rougemont and Harlsey.

This is primarily a walking book. The aim is to link castles with footpaths through interesting and pleasant countryside. This has not always been possible, however. Where footpaths do not conveniently link sites, roads have had to be used. This has been kept to a minimum and extra care must be taken when walking down or across roads.

Information is given on each of the castle sites visited, and on other historic sites. The book can, therefore, be used as local history book, but the information is not in any way meant to be definitive. There is far more to learn about each site and simply not enough room here for more than just a brief outline of the history of each of the sites visited.

Each walk is circular and begins – and ends – at a pub in a small village. Should you wish to partake of their hospitality on the completion of your walk, make sure you know what the pub has to offer and whether or not it will be open on your return. Pubs are important, not because all walkers are boozers, but because most good modern public houses and inns provide a whole range of sustenance, from hot drinks and light snacks, to full meals, soft drinks and beer. Pubs also provide shelter from the elements, plus toilets and telephones should they be needed. It is hoped that all the pubs and inns mentioned in this book will greet walkers with a warm and friendly welcome. However, the pubs have been chosen as starting/finishing points purely on their location within a convenient village.

Each walk heads off in an anti-clockwise direction but one could start from any point along the route. IT IS IMPORTANT TO NOTE that all walks are intended as FULL DAY walks and are not to be mistaken for gentle 'afternoon strolls'. Be prepared.

Check the weather before setting off, too. The moors will be snowbound in winter while the low river valleys are often subject to flooding. See www.metoffice.com for local forecasts.

It is also important to note that not all castles mentioned in the text are open to the public. Some are on private land and the privacy of the owners should be respected at all times. Of those that are open, some are restricted by certain hours or by season. Some charge for entry, so check details before setting off to avoid disappointment.

The author accepts no responsibility for inclement weather, nettle stings, barking farm dogs, boisterous cattle, flooded streams, footpath obstructions, local detours, flat beer or noisy coach parties.

The time taken to complete each walk will depend upon the fitness of the walker, and how much time is spent enjoying the views, stopping for lunch and exploring sites along the way. Distances have been measured using a *Recta* measuring wheel on the relevant Ordnance Survey Explorer 1:25,000 series maps. The inaccuracies of such a method must be taken into account. NB: ALL DISTANCES QUOTED SHOULD BE TAKEN AS APPROXIMATE. It is advisable to take the relevant OS map with you, as indicated at the beginning of each Castle Walk.

The aim of this guide is to direct walkers along an interesting route that will take in points of ecological, geological, geographical and historical interest, and take in at least one castle site. Examples of flora and fauna are included, although this is by no means meant to be the definitive list. It should be noted that the time of year and weather conditions will dictate what plants and birds are seen due to natural, migrational and seasonal patterns. Plants, animals and birds are only mentioned in areas where they can be seen. Inclusion is not arbitrary.

In a guide of this nature there is no room to explain every feature or its value in full, but it is hoped that each entry will generate an

The massive keep at the heart of Middleham Castle.

interest for people to follow up at a later date. Details of the castles and castle sites are deliberately brief. Explore at your leisure.

Any comments to the author will be welcome, by e-mailing Peter Williamson at auctor@supanet.com.

As the walks venture from lowland estuary to Limestone Dale and high North Yorkshire Moor, it is advisable to take precautions regarding clothing and equipment carried on each section, including something to eat and drink. Always wear sensible boots and take waterproofs – this is, after all, Yorkshire.

Always follow The Countryside Code . . .

- Enjoy the countryside and respect its life and work;
- Leave livestock, crops and machinery alone;
- Guard against all risks of fire;
- Take your litter home;
- Fasten all gates;
- Respect the property and wishes of landowners;
- Help to keep all water clean;
- If you must take a dog, keep it on a lead, and always clean up after it;
- Protect wildlife, trees and plants;
- Keep to public paths across farmland;
- Take special care on country roads;
- Use gates and stiles to cross fences, hedges and walls;
- Make no unnecessary noise.

Whatever your experience or ability, *Castles Walks in Yorkshire* has been devised and written to provide hours of healthy exercise and enjoyable walking through the stunning scenery and rich heritage of Britain's biggest and best-loved county.

NB – for anyone not capable of walking the full length of these walks, it may be possible to visit some of these sites by car. Several stand by roadsides or require a short stroll to reach. Therefore, use this book as a local history guide to direct you to wherever takes your fancy. You will not be disappointed . . .

Introduction

Yorkshire is a great county, full of diverse geographical interest and historical intrigue. Castles once proliferated, from the Tees in the north to the Don in the south, from the Wharfe in the west to the Humber in the east. Today, the remains of many of these once mighty structures are still visible, although the nature of those ruins varies enormously.

It is commonly accepted that castles as we know them were first introduced into this country after the Norman Conquest of 1066. As William 'the Bastard' (he was the illegitimate son of Robert, Duke of Normandy, and a tanner's daughter) sought to control his newly conquered lands, he gave control of the regions to his battle captains who began a campaign of castle-building from where they could subjugate the local peasant population. As the Anglo-Saxon Chronicles state, 'they built castles widely throughout this nation and oppressed the wretched people.'

In order to speed up this operation, earthen structures were hurriedly thrown up across the land, known as 'motte and bailey' forts or castles. In simple terms, a mound of earth (the 'motte') was erected by piling up layers of earth and stones from a deep ditch dug around it. The motte would then be surrounded by an enclosure (the 'bailey'), which in turn was surrounded by an earthen rampart and ditch. A wooden stockade would be erected around the whole perimeter on the rampart and a timber tower erected on the motte.

It was from the tower that the castle owner could survey the outlying lands, as well as being a refuge should the castle be attacked. Once the defensive elements were in place, storehouses, stables, kitchens, workshops and a great hall could be built within the bailey.

By counting the number of mottes that exist in England today, it has been estimated that the Normans built around 500 such castles in England between 1066 and 1086. They were symbols of the might and authority of Norman rule, and this became even more obvious when the wooden structures were gradually replaced with stone on many, but not all, sites.

Many of England's best-known castles started off as motte and bailey constructions, made of timber and earth. However, once the immediate need to build castles had been quickly met, their owners soon turned to rebuilding in stone. Edward I was probably the most prolific castle builder in Britain, as he strengthened his borders with mighty fortresses or dominated his dominions with powerful stone symbols of his absolute and supreme authority.

At the time of the Civil Wars of the mid-seventeenth century many castles were ordered to be 'slighted', or damaged so that enemy garrisons could no longer operate from within strong walls. Many have remained ruinous; some were later remodelled; and others have vanished completely. As the kingdom gradually became more peaceful, and weapons more powerful, the strategic importance of castles declined and many were converted into grand country homes.

This book, therefore, contains walks to sites that show the evolution of castles in Yorkshire. Walkers can visit abandoned earthworks (Rougemont), short-lived earthen mottes (Carlton and Mulgrave), stone-built motte and baileys (Pickering and Sandal), massive fortresses (Middleham and Scarborough), fortified towers (West Tanfield and Paull), hunting lodges (Barden) and grand houses (Mortham and Snape).

Whatever their current state, all are fascinating and exciting sites that evoke images of knights in armour and battles between king and country. Immerse yourself in the history of this great county and enjoy some truly wonderful castle walks in Yorkshire.

Castles, manors, towers and ruins in Yorkshire

The following is an alphabetical list with numbers 1–176 which relate to the map of Yorkshire overleaf. The list includes castles, fortified manors and towers, ruins and the earthworks of the same.

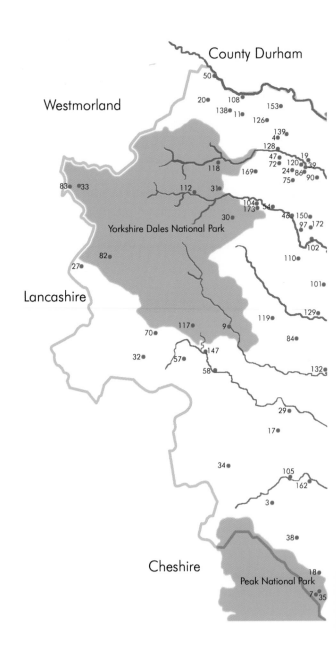

County Durham

Westmorland

50

20   108
138 11   153
126

139
4
128
47   19
72   120   39
24 86
75   90

118

169

83   33

112   31

104
173   54
46   150
97   172

30

102

Yorkshire Dales National Park

110

82

101

27

Lancashire

129

119

117   9

84

70

32

57   147

58

132

29

17

34

105
162

3

38

Cheshire

18

Peak National Park

7   35

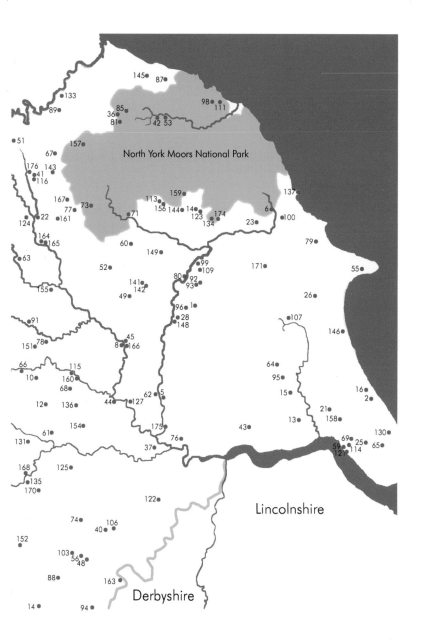

North York Moors National Park

Lincolnshire

Derbyshire

Sandal Castle, Walton Hall's Watergate and Wakefield Motte

22 km/13.5 miles

Explorer OL278 *Sheffield and Barnsley*

Start from the Fox and Hounds in Newmillerdam

The village of Newmillerdam (New-mill-on-the-dam) stands at the head of a large millpond that was once part of the Chevet Park Estate.

From the public 'pay and display' car park opposite the Fox and Hounds public house at the head of Newmillerdam on the Barnsley Road A61, take the woodland footpath through the trees up the right-hand side of the lake, keeping left at the first fork. Pass through the gateway and keep the lake on the immediate left. This is Newmillerdam Country Park.

The Park (a Site of Special Scientific Interest, SSSI) covers some 237 acres of woodland and water and was originally managed for game and supplies of wood, with pine and larch having been planted to provide timber for pit props.

Continue along the red shale path and, after a short distance, the elegant Georgian boathouse can be seen across the lake.

The boathouse was built by William Pilkington, c.1826, and was used by the Pilkington family to entertain guests throughout the nineteenth and early twentieth centuries. While the gentlemen were out shooting the wildfowl on the lake, the ladies would adjourn to the boathouse, where a picnic lunch was served. The

1

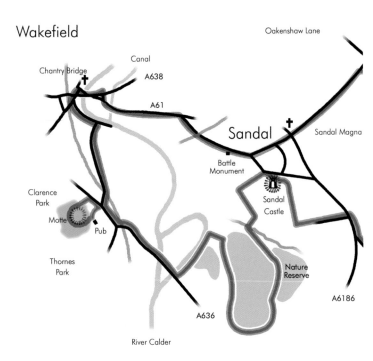

Wakefield

Oakenshaw Lane

Canal

Chantry Bridge

A638

A61

Sandal

Sandal Magna

Battle
Monument

Clarence
Park

Sandal
Castle

Motte

Pub

Thornes
Park

Nature
Reserve

A6186

A636

River Calder

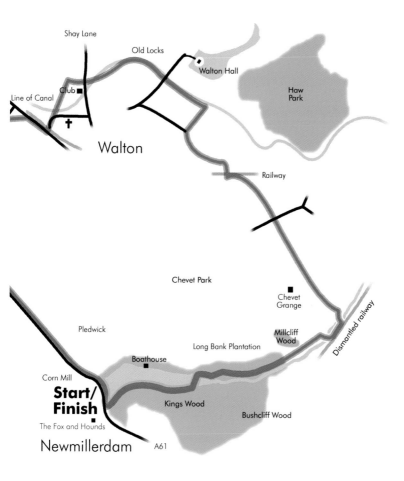

Shay Lane

Old Locks

Walton Hall

Haw
Park

Line of Canal

Club

Walton

Railway

Chevet Park

Chevet
Grange

Dismantled railway

Pledwick

Millcliff
Wood

Long Bank Plantation

Boathouse

Corn Mill
**Start/
Finish**
The Fox and Hounds

Kings Wood

Bushcliff Wood

Newmillerdam

A61

The Pilkington boathouse of 1826.

Grade II Listed building was restored in 1999 and now houses a visitor facility and meeting room.

Continue through the trees to where the path forks left to a concrete walkway and footbridge across the lake.

The lake is an important breeding site for great crested grebe, moorhen and coot, and herons can regularly be seen feeding in the shallow water. Canada geese are also regular visitors calling in to share this watery habitat with the resident mallard.

Once across the water, turn right and continue straight ahead, climbing into the wood.

The mature beech beside the lake were planted by the Pilkington family to provide cover for game birds, whilst the rest of the woods contain a mixture of larch, pine, oak, sycamore, beech and silver birch. Today, several areas are being thinned to allow the mixed deciduous woodland to mature, and to improve the wildlife habitat.

Keep ahead along the woodland path, and, after a short distance, a wooden stile leads into open fields.

These woods are home to much wildlife, including grey squirrel, rabbit and fox, as well as great spotted woodpecker, wren, thrush, robin, tree creeper, long-tailed tit and sparrowhawk.

Walk ahead through the field dropping down to meet the marshy tree-lined banks of Bushcliff Beck on the right.

The marshy areas support a great variety of plants, like water mint, meadowsweet, marsh marigold and creeping buttercup. Alder, willow and great tussock sedge line the beck and, where the marsh has dried out, reed grass and nettles grow on the edge of the woodland.

Once beside the stream the path takes a small stone arch bridge over the beck, now called Bleakley Dike, and then turns sharp left. Continue down the valley following the stream. After a short distance the path turns sharp right and goes directly up the hill to the old railway embankment.

The Midland Railway Company's Chevet Branch Railway Line was part of a Leeds bypass scheme and was mainly used for freight, although a passenger service between Halifax and Sheffield began in 1909. The line closed in 1968, and today it is a permissive bridleway for horse riders, cyclists and walkers.

At the banking take the wooden steps that lead round to the left. Keep left along the banking with the line of the old railway down to the right in a heavily overgrown cutting. Pass the bridge over the old track on the right – do not cross it – and keep straight ahead. Where the path swings down to the right to join the old railway, keep straight ahead through the undergrowth until reaching a wooden marker post by a line of small oak trees.

During the summer months, the banks here are covered in the pink flowers of Himalayan balsam, which grows in wild abundance along many railway lines. Its 'exploding' seedpods can come as quite a shock.

At the post, go down a couple of steps and then head straight back down the field to the stream.

Many butterflies can be seen on the poppies and mayweed in these fields, most notably the small tortoiseshell, the wall brown and the large white.

A wide wooden bridge crosses the first stream, after which the path bears right to a small meadow. After a short distance take the path over the stream on the left and keep left into the corner of the field to a marker post by the wall.

The streams are lined with crack willow and hawthorn, whilst bulrush and the unmistakable cigar-like flower spikes of great reedmace flourish in the shallow water.

Follow the wall away from the stream, passing Chevet Grange on the way out to Chevet Lane.

This wall marks the boundary of the Chevet Hall Estate that once covered 2,340 acres. The original house was built in 1529 by the Neville family, but was demolished during the 1960s. In 1753 the Pilkington family bought the estate and used it for hunting and fishing. Nine lodges were built around the perimeter of the estate in the 1890s to house the many gamekeepers who fought a constant battle with poachers.

The wide green path continues beside the wall for 1km (just over half a mile), passing through fields of cabbage and rhubarb, where pheasant, grouse and lapwing take advantage of the cover.

Wakefield soil is ideal for rhubarb and the town celebrates a rhubarb festival each year in February. The plant

The footpath past Chevet Grange.

was introduced into England in the eighteenth century by Henry Baker, son-in-law of writer Daniel Defoe.

At Chevet Lane cross directly over the road as indicated by signs. Walk along the path between fence and hawthorn hedge climbing two stiles on the way to the railway cutting ahead. Just before the railway, take a stile into the corner of the field. Turn left up the tree line and then head through the brambles on the right to a footbridge over the railway.

This is just one of many hundreds of branch lines that once criss-crossed this area, taking coal from the once thriving coal pits to join the national railway network. It was opened in 1840 by the North Midland Railway, and today it is used as a freight line and as a test track for new trains.

Head left up the bank and then strike out across the field towards the solitary oak tree. The tree marks the beginning of an old boundary that heads out across the fields

Haw Park Wood (an SSSI) was originally part of a much larger wooded area that once included Hare Wood. Both names derive from the Saxon hay, meaning 'hunting ground' or 'fenced park'. A small area is believed to be ancient woodland where fox, weasel, stoat and badger can be found.

Follow the path along the old field boundary to a track and, at the gate, pass through onto the road. Turn right and follow the lane (Sike Lane) down to the old Barnsley Canal.

Prior to the railways, the Barnsley Canal was built to transport coal from the north Barnsley area to the Aire & Calder Navigation. (The canals or navigations gave rise to the term 'navvy' for the workers who built the canals.) Work began in June 1793, but today, sadly having fallen into disuse, the canal is overgrown with trees and covered in green algae.

Just before the bridge turn left, and follow the path through the woods down to the towpath, although at this point there is no water in the canal. Follow the canal towpath along to the left. This is part of the Trans Pennine Trail.

The Trans-Pennine Trail is a 350-mile national route crossing the country from east to west, and from north to south. It has been created for the enjoyment of walkers, cyclists and horse riders.

Follow the towpath along, passing beneath a bridge that leads into the grounds of Walton Hall, now a hotel.

The original house was first recorded in 1334 but, in 1767, Thomas Waterton demolished the old hall and built the present Georgian mansion on the island in the lake. All that remains of the medieval house is the ivy-covered Water Gate. In the nineteenth century Walton Hall was the home of Charles Waterton, pioneering naturalist and traveller, who created what was effectively the world's first nature reserve at Walton Park. Of particular note in the gardens is a unique stone sundial, by Boulby of Crofton, constructed in 1813.

Continue along the towpath, passing the remains of two overgrown locks.

Between Wakefield and Barnsley the canal had twenty locks positioned to keep the flow of water constant. At Walton there were twelve locks, although the remains of only two can be seen today. The last boat sailed down the canal in 1952.

After a short distance the canal disappears under dense undergrowth. From here it has been filled in, although the path continues to follow its course.

Walton (farmstead of the Britons) is a small village once belonging to the Manor of Walton. A mainly rural area, the village grew with the Industrial Revolution when the canal and then the railway arrived. During the nineteenth century the village had five schools and six public alehouses.

Follow the path as it swings round to the left between back garden fences. The houses are built on the site of the old Walton soap works.

In 1832, Edward Simpson established a soapworks in Soap House Yard, but widespread pollution soon threatened the surrounding countryside, causing Charles Waterton of Walton Hall and Sir William Pilkington of Chevet Park to band together

The medieval Watergate, Walton Hall.

in protest in 1846. Simpson was later to buy Walton Hall in 1876.

At the road (Shay Lane) turn right, but then cross immediately to take the footpath down the side of Walton Sports and Social Club car park. Follow the path to the stile at the bottom of the hedge and houses, and then turn left to follow the bottom of the sports ground, with an open field on the right.

The meadow is awash with colour in the summer months when redleg, or redshank, in particular, turns the fields pink.

In the corner of the field, go through the gap onto a cinder track. Go straight ahead (due west) and follow the track over a small bridge into the corner of School Lane.

This is a stranded canal bridge over the now filled-in Barnsley Canal that once ran through this field on its way north. Up to the left is the fourteenth-century church of St Peter, with its Norman tower and Jacobean pulpit.

At the road, walk straight ahead past the post office and under the railway bridges. Turn right. Follow the road (Oakenshaw Lane) for a short distance to a footpath sign on the left. Take the path between the houses to come out in a field heading towards Sandal.

Ridge and furrow plough marks, off Manygates Lane.

In medieval times, Sandal (sandy nook of land) would have been a small community centred on the church of St Helen, and was dominated and protected by Sandal Castle. Fields and dense woodland once surrounded the village.

Cross the field to the right, aiming directly for the tall spire of Wakefield parish church, to meet the road (Walton Lane) by a bridge over a stream. Turn left and walk up the road to Sandal Magna.

When Daniel Defoe visited the area in the early eighteenth century, he wrote: 'Wakefield is a clean, large, well-built town, very populous and very rich; here is a very large church, well filled it is, for here there are few Dissenters; the steeple is a very fine spire, by far the highest in all this part of the country.' All Saints' Church in Wakefield was raised to cathedral status in 1888.

Follow the dinosaur's footprints to the traffic lights, at which point St Helen's Church is down to the right.

Dedicated to St Helen (the mother of the Roman emperor Constantine) the parish church in Sandal dates from c.1091–7. Two churches in the area are mentioned in the Domesday Book of 1086, and it is assumed that one is St Helen's. No trace now remains of the original church, but sections of the piers of the later church built c.1150 indicate that the present church occupies the same position. In the fourteenth century the church was rebuilt, and a major restoration took place in 1872 when the Victorians tried to recreate the original medieval splendour.

Cross straight over the main road (Barnsley Road, A61) and continue along Castle Road to the junction. Turn right and walk down Manygates Lane to the main road.

After a short distance on the left is a school. Within the roadside railings stands a simple monument erected on the spot where the Duke of York was slain at the Battle of Wakefield on 30 December 1460. This monument of 1897 replaces one that was demolished during the Civil War. Across the road on Wakefield Green – the only part of the battlefield which remains undeveloped – are signs of medieval 'ridge and furrow' ploughing.

Pass under the railway bridge and turn left down the main road (A61) opposite the Foresters' Arms.

The Battle of Wakefield was the fifth set-piece battle within the Wars of the Roses, 1455–87. Despite being heavily out-numbered, Richard Plantagenet, Duke of York, left the protective walls of Sandal Castle to attack the Lancastrian army of King Henry VI near Wakefield Bridge. Both Richard and his son were slain, and the episode was immortalized by William Shakespeare in Henry VI, Part 3. *The Wars of the Roses rumbled on for several more years, before Richard III was killed at the Battle of Bosworth Field by Henry Tudor in 1485.*

Continue down the main road, crossing over to the other side where it crosses the canal or 'cut'.

This section of canal is the Fall Ings Cut, opened in the 1760s as part of the Aire & Calder Navigation. In the 1850s, a boatyard occupied the site between Bridge Street and Doncaster Road, from where the Ann Turgoose, *the largest ship ever built in*

11

The Aire & Calder Navigation, Wakefield.

Wakefield, was launched in 1855. This two-masted schooner carried on its maiden voyage Bradford-made cannonballs to the British Army in the Crimea.

Just before the road widens at the junction of the A16 and A638, turn right and walk straight ahead behind the bus shelter. Use the pedestrian crossings to walk over the carriageways directly ahead towards a car showroom on the A638. Once over the road, turn left and walk ahead past the old packhorse bridge, and then cross the old chantry bridge over the River Calder.

The chantry chapel of St Mary-on-the-bridge was built between 1342 and 1356 and is one of only four bridge chapels still surviving in England. The chapel was first licensed in 1356 but services were cancelled in 1548 after which it was let as a commercial building. It suffered almost 300 years of neglect but was eventually restored in 1847 and rededicated in 1848. The original front was used as a boathouse for Kettlethorpe Hall. Daniel Defoe visited the chapel c.1712 and noted, 'The Calder passes through [Wakefield] under a stately stone bridge of twelve arches, upon which is famous building, by some called a chapel, by others a castle, the former is most likely. It was built by Edward IV in memory of the fatal Battle of Wakefield, when his father, Richard, Duke of York, was killed.'

Once over the river, turn left to rejoin the main road.

Over to the right is a small, single-storey stone building of 1850 that once housed the offices of the Aire & Calder Navigation Company, founded in 1699. In the seventeenth century, many 'navigations' were built, whereby channels (with locks) were cut to join sections of navigable river.

Turn right and walk under the huge railway bridge to the pedestrian crossing beyond the Grey Horse pub. Cross the main road and then left again to walk back under the railway bridge and over the 'slip' road to the river once more.

The 'new' bridge was opened in 1933 to alleviate congestion on the chantry bridge. Several mills and houses had to be demolished to make room for the wide road.

Just before the 'new' road bridge, turn right and follow the path to Thornes Lane. Turn left and follow the lane all the way to the end, as it swings right and then left, passing under the railway twice more before it meets the main road (A636). At the roundabout turn right to a red telephone box just after the Thornes parish church of St James. Cross the dual carriageway, and walk ahead up the path into Clarence Park passing a commemorative horse trough of 1888 and a drinking fountain of 1898 on the way up the hill.

The chantry chapel of St Mary-on-the-bridge.

The wooded motte in Clarence Park.

In 1890, C. G. Milnes-Gaskill of Thornes House gave land for a public park, including the earthworks motte on Lawe Hill. The following year, the Duke of Clarence planted a white horse chestnut tree to inaugurate the park, which was formally opened on 6 July 1893.

Go up the horse-chestnut-lined path to where it levels off. At this point, turn left and walk straight up the hill towards the wooded motte. Half way up the hill, follow the path that leads round to the right with a distinctive ditch and the motte on the left.

The neighbouring estates of Holmfield and Thornes Parks were added to Clarence Park after the First World War.

After almost circumnavigating the motte, take the path that leads down towards the large house on the right. This path winds beneath a massive tree to the car park of the Holmfield Arms. Turn left and walk down the hill, back to the roundabout on the main road. Just before the road take the path on the right.

Wakefield Castle is an interesting earthwork motte and bailey fortress. The tree-covered motte still has its surrounding ditch and two baileys, which lie in-line to the north-east of the motte. There are traces of the outer ditch around the baileys but the site is surrounded by trees and hedges and is, therefore, best viewed in the winter.

Follow this path to the pedestrian crossing and cross the main road on the left. Turn right and follow the road under the railway bridge and over the Calder & Hebble Navigation and the River Calder. Once over the bridge, take the path beside the river immediately on the left.

Wakefield (open land where festivals, or wakes, take place) was part of lands granted to the Earls of Warenne in the twelfth century. Some time before 1157, the Earls of Warenne decided to build a castle at Sandal Magna to take advantage of its position overlooking the River Calder.

Walk ahead along the embankment with the river on the left, and a small reedy pond on the right. The embankment soon veers to the right, away from the river, and leads to the path that circles a large lake.

Pugneys Country Park consists of three lakes, which were reclaimed from old quarries in the 1970s. One is a designated nature reserve.

Turn right and walk all around the lake, passing between the main water sports lake and the nature reserve. Having almost completed a full circle of the main lake, take the footpath over the small wooded stream, Pugney's Drain, on the right.

Bird species sighted here have included mute swan, Canada goose, tufted duck, mallard, coot, cormorant, grey heron, wigeon, great crested grebe, pochard, ruddy duck, black headed gull, lapwing, redshank, goldeneye, golden plover, pied wagtail and herring gull.

The path goes right and then veers left up the field with the castle ahead. At the lane, turn left and walk up to the corner of the housing estate, now with the castle on the right. Turn right and follow the path all the way up to Manygates Lane. Turn right and enter the grounds of Sandal Castle.

> *Several packhorse routes ran through Sandal, until the mid-eighteenth century when roads were being turned into turnpikes. Gates were strategically placed in side roads to stop people evading the payment of tolls, hence the name of Manygates Lane.*

Walk through the castle grounds past the visitor centre/shop, and take the stile on the left. Walk along behind the houses and then turn right at the hedge. Follow the path down the hill to Castle Farm with Emley Moor mast in the far distance.

Sandal Castle is an impressive stone motte and bailey fortress, which was left uncovered after excavation. The stonework dates from 1190, and it is thought to have been built for the Earl de Warenne by Hamelin Plantagenet who built Conisbrough Castle. In the wide outer ditch are the foundations of the gatehouse, with fragments of the hall, a large well and other foundations in the bailey. A substantial inner barbican, within its own ditch, guards the central keep which

The ruins of Sandal Castle.

once adorned the motte. There are fine views across Wakefield from the top, including a glimpse of the earlier, tree-covered Wakefield motte.

Follow the fence to the left around the buildings and take the stile into the lane. Turn left. Follow this lane (Milnthorpe Lane) all the way to the main road. Turn right.

Up to the left is the Three Houses Inn, an old coaching inn. During the seventeenth century, coaching inns thrived through passing trade – as did highwaymen. One, John Nevison, was spectacularly captured asleep on a chair in the old Three Houses Inn, Sandal, in 1684.

Cross the main road by the Walnut Tree public house and then take the left-hand fork (A61 Barnsley Road) signposted to Newmillerdam Country Park. After a short distance the road passes a row of quaint Victorian almshouses.

Erected in 1883, 'Harrison's Homes for the Aged Poor' were financed by local barrister, Samuel Fozard Harrison, and built for 'deserving poor persons of either sex, either married or single, residing at the time of the election in the parish of Sandal'. Designed by architect Fred Simpson, the brief was to be the 'free adoption of the classic style of the popular Renaissance period'. They have since been converted into three small detached homes.

Cross the dam wall with the old corn mill on the right and the car park is in the trees on the left.

The first mill was built in the area in about 1285 and a dam built to provide waterpower. This was one of only three soke mills within the manor of Wakefield, built by the Lord of the Manor, the Earl de Warenne. At a 'soke' mill the estate's tenants were allowed to grind their corn in a return for a proportion of the ground grain, or 'mouter' (flour). In 1653 a 'new' mill was built on the turnpike and the dammed lake increased in size. The current building was built in the 1820s by Francis Neville of Chevet Hall and was in use until 1960.

Tickhill and Conisbrough Castles

29 km/18 miles

Explorer 279 *Doncaster – Conisbrough, Maltby and Thorne*

Start from the Three Tuns in Stainton

A 'tun' is a large beer cask holding 252 gallons, or 2,016 pints. Three tuns, therefore, hold 6,048 pints, which should be enough to keep the locals happy for a short while!

From the pub, go up School Lane, and follow this quiet country road around to the left, passing St Winifred's Church on the right.

> *St Winifred's Church stands in the centre of old Stainton (farmstead on stony ground). The church contains a Norman chancel arch from 1290, interesting stained glass, and two carved heads from the fifteenth century.*

At the junction turn right down Lime Kiln Lane.

> *Limekilns were built in areas where carboniferous limestone was to be found to save carting. The limestone was burned with coal to make a fine alkali powder (quicklime) that reduced the acidity of the soil. The remains of these stone furnaces can still be seen in some places.*

About 100 metres after the railway bridge, with the working Maltby Colliery over fields on the right, turn left at the footpath sign. Cross the track over the stream and then turn left, following the straggly hedge along the bottom of the field.

> *The stream is well hidden by willow, ash, hawthorn, nettles and butterbur, the huge leaves of which are a common sight in summer and early autumn on many riverbanks.*

St Winifred's church, Stainton.

After a short distance a marker post indicates where the path heads into the undergrowth on the left. Follow the winding path between young beech and oak trees until it arrives at an open field. A sign on the post indicates that this is part of the Danum Trail.

> *The Danum Trail is a series of walks linking villages and townships in the Doncaster Metropolitan Borough. Together these linear walks make up an 80km/50 mile leisure trail, designed primarily for walking in sections and readily accessible by public transport. The official starting point is the Dome Leisure Park and the walk finishes at the Glass Park, Kirk Sandal.*

Maltby Colliery.

The trail is waymarked with the symbol of a Roman centurion soldier indicating the area's Roman connections.

Head out across the field, just to the left of the large pylon, and pass through a gap in the far hedge.

Game birds abound in these fields. The partridge is native to England but it was the Normans who introduced the pheasant in the eleventh century as a food source.

Go through the hedge and cross this field into the opposite bottom corner where the trees lining the stream meet the path at a marker post. Climb the stile and cross the small wooden bridge, known as Denaby Wife Bridge.

The large rhubarb-like leaves of the butterbur were once used to wrap butter, hence its name. Its distinctive small lilac-pink flowers cluster on large spikes from February to April, and the leaves form great thickets in summer.

Continue along the bottom of the field and, after a short distance, cross the stream on the left and then head up the field towards the end of a hedge beneath the pylons. Turn right and follow the track beneath the cables until reaching the lane. Turn right down Hindley Lane with the tower of Harworth Colliery ahead in the distance.

This area of Yorkshire was once the powerhouse of Britain with busy collieries dotting the landscape. Sadly, these have all but gone now as alternative forms of energy have led to the virtual death of Yorkshire's once-proud mining industry, and the traditional communities it supported.

After a short distance the track turns left to meet Apy Hill Lane. Turn right and follow the road under the railway into Tickhill. Opposite the first house, turn right down Stoney Lane to the main road (A631) beside Friary Farm.

Across the road are the remains of an Austin Friary, founded in c.1260. These are somewhat difficult to identify as most have been incorporated into later houses, although a thirteenth century decorated 'dog-tooth' arch still stands in one garden. The simple Augustinian Rule for monastic life was adopted by a group of friars in 1256, after which they became known as the Austin Friars.

Turn left and head into Tickhill along Rotherham Road, which soon becomes Westgate.

The Honour of Tickhill was given to Roger de Busli as a reward for his part in the Norman Invasion of England, although when he built the castle here the Saxon settlement was known as Dadesley. The name 'Tickhill' first appeared in the twelfth century and is probably derived from a local landowner, as in 'Tica's Hill'.

Cross Worksop Road, and then turn right down a footpath just after No. 71. Cross the stream to a road called simply 'Lindrick'. Turn left and where Lindrick joins Lindrick Lane, turn left again. Follow the millrace, lined with willow, to the millpond.

There has been a mill on this site since the fourteenth century, although the present mill was built in the eighteenth century. At the end of the millpond is Rowland's Bridge, a thirteenth, century clapper bridge built from a single block of locally quarried magnesium limestone.

Go ahead up the ramp beside the weir and follow the paved path around to the right with pond on the left. Behind the wall on the right is Tickhill Castle.

Tickhill Castle is an early Norman motte and bailey castle. The first stone section was the eleventh-century gatehouse, which

The motte, Tickhill Castle.

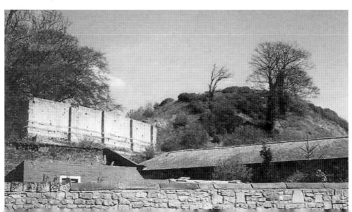

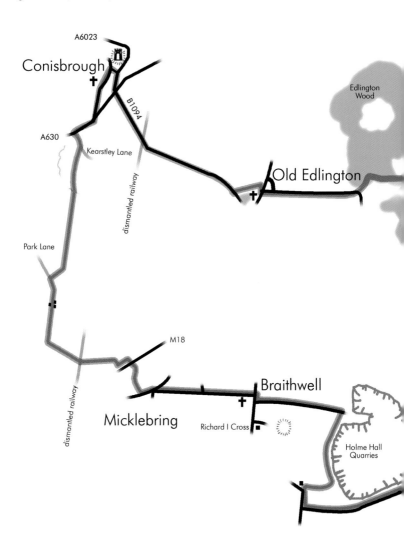

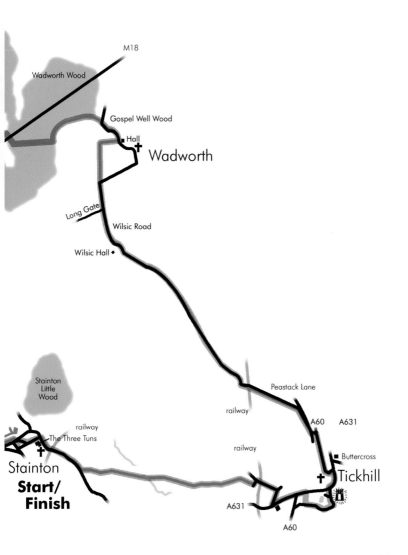

incorporated the drawbridge over the wet moat. It is one of the oldest surviving Norman gatehouses in England. On the 75ft-high motte stood the ten-sided keep built by Henry II in 1178–79. The curtain wall, also of the twelfth century, was built atop a massive earlier rampart that is surrounded by a 30ft-wide ditch.

For a better view, turn right and walk back around the bottom end of the wall along a public footpath into the farmyard. Over the wall can be seen the motte and part of the castle's stone inner curtain wall.

In his travels across England in the 1530s and '40s, Tudor scholar John Leland visited Tickhill, describing the castle as 'well defended by a ditch, and a wall built from masonry of a very hard and dark stone. The keep is the finest portion of the castle, and apart from an old hall all the buildings within the castle precinct have been demolished'.

Walk back up Castle Gate to the main road, and turn right at the Millstone pub. Follow Castle Gate round into the town centre.

In the centre of the town stands the market cross (Buttercross) and St Leonard's Hospital, now the parish rooms.

Turn left down St Mary's Gate, signposted to the parish church.

Leland also commented that Tickhill was 'a very impoverished market town, although it has a fine, large church.' The church of St Mary probably dates from the thirteenth century, although rebuilding took place from 1340. The

The Buttercross, Tickhill.

tower and main body of the church are battlemented and there are examples of heraldry around the walls. Inside is the alabaster tomb of Thomas Fitzwilliam formerly in the Friary. Pevsner calls it 'the proudest parish church in the West Riding, except for those of the big towns'.

At the church turn right, up St Mary's Road, which becomes Wilsic Lane. The road turns left and then, at the junction with Wong Lane, right, although this is still Wilsic Lane.

'Wong' relates to a section of 'low-lying enclosed land among open strips, often marshy'. Wilsic Lane is a quiet unenclosed country lane that leads all the way to the small hamlet of Wilsic, with large wide arable fields on both sides.

Keep on the road past Home Farm and continue through the buildings passing Wilsic Hall, now a school, on the left.

Wilsic Hall School occupies 18 acres of beautiful grounds, and provides accommodation, education and therapeutic services for people with severe challenging behaviour resulting from autism or severe learning difficulties.

After a short distance Wilsic Road reaches Long Gate. Go straight ahead at the junction and follow the road towards Wadworth. Where the road turns right, go ahead down Green Lane crossing Short Gate after a few metres. After half a mile turn right at the footpath sign and cross two fields to the village of Wadworth. Climb the stile at the road and turn left.

In Wadworth (enclosure of a man called Wada) is the Church of St John the Baptist, founded c.1300. Of particular note under the south wall is the recumbent effigy of a knight in hunting dress, which is unique in Yorkshire.

Walk down the road past Wadworth Hall.

Wadworth Hall is reached by passing between two substantial lodges, and is a dramatic design of three bays with a Venetian central window.

Just beyond the high wall of the hall grounds, turn right into the wood.

This is Gospel Well Wood, owned by the Woodland Trust, the UK's leading conservation charity, which is dedicated to the protection of Britain's native woodland heritage. Since the Trust was founded in 1972 it has grown to care and protect over 1,000 sites covering 17,500 hectares (43,000 acres). A 'gospel well' or 'gospel tree' was generally that which marked the boundary of a parish or a manor.

Follow the path to the left along the top of woods, until a second opening which leads back out onto the road. Go ahead at the crossroads along Wood House Lane but, where it turns right into Wadworth Wood, keep ahead and follow the outside of the wood as it swings round to the left. Where the footpath comes in from the left across the fields, turn right into the wood.

The blackberry, or bramble, is one of the commonest plants in Britain, thriving in woodlands such as this. It produces an abundant supply of edible berries, whilst the leaves have been used to treat wounds and as an ingredient in herbal fruit teas. When St Michael threw the devil out of heaven, Lucifer landed right in the middle of a bramble bush. Such was his anger, that he returns every year to blight the humble bramble on Michaelmas Day, 29 September, after which the picking season traditionally ends.

Follow the path in a straight line down through the woods to the second junction. Turn right and follow the path beneath the M18 motorway. In the wood take the left fork in the main path. (Do not turn sharp left beside the motorway.) Follow this path through the bracken beneath beech, sycamore and oak trees to a large clearing. Go left and, at the corner of the fenced section, continue straight ahead, back into the depths of the wood.

Up to the right in this wood (Edlington Wood) are ancient earthworks and enclosures for those with time to explore.

At the next junction in the path, turn left and follow the track to the road, Wood Lane. Turn right and follow the sunken lane into Old Edlington.

Old Edlington (enclosure of a man called Edla) is the original village here, as opposed to New Edlington, a more modern mining village. In Old English, the Saxon name would have been pronounced 'Aethling-tun', although spelt 'Aeðlingtun'. The ð was pronounced 'th', and was written like a lower case 'd' with a cross bar through the ascender. However, uneducated or careless transcriptions over time have corrupted the name to what we see today.

Follow the lane all the way to the main road. Cross the B6376 and take the footpath along Rectory Gardens below the church.

St Peter's Church contains many Norman features, including the nave and chancel and a fine door inside the porch. A coffin plate commemorates Philip Whorton who was Warden of the Mint in the mid-seventeenth century.

Follow the fenced-off path along the top of the field to the road (B6094). Turn right and follow this road (Carr Lane) all the way down to the traffic lights on the Sheffield Road (A630). Go straight over at the lights and follow Low Road round to the right. The towering ruins of Conisbrough Castle soon appear on the left. Turn up the hill just before the memorial garden.

The lamp and fountain was erected by public subscription to commemorate the coronation of George V in June 1911.

St Peter's Church, Edlington.

The magnificent Conisbrough Castle.

After a short distance go through the metal kissing gate on the right to explore the castle before leaving by the main gate.

The keep at Conisbrough Castle is one of the finest medieval buildings in the country. The site comprises an impressive stone motte and bailey, with a unique twelfth-century great circular buttressed keep. The enormous motte, which holds the inner bailey, is a natural mound, strongly scarped and ditched. The high curtain wall surrounds the keep and the foundations of various domestic buildings in the inner bailey, and a curved outer bailey lies beyond the gatehouse and angled barbican. Leland commented that the castle 'standeth on a rocket of stone and ditched. The walls of it are strong and full of towers.'

Turn left briefly down the hill and then right along Castle Avenue, passing the Terrace Café. Cross over New Hill onto March Street and then turn left down Church Lane passing the Wesleyan Chapel of 1876.

Conisbrough Castle was used as a setting in Sir Walter Scott's ballad, Ivanhoe, *a tale of chivalry, set in the age of Richard I. In this medieval tale, Wilfred of Ivanhoe loves a maiden called Rowena, but she is promised to Athelstane of Conisbrough. Ivanhoe ends up fighting for King Richard against his brother John, but wins the day and the hand of the fair Rowena.*

At the end of the road cross straight over March Gate and keep ahead along Hollywell Lane, following it down and round to join the main road.

The town centre of Conisbrough (the king's fortification) is up to the right on a high scarp overlooking the river Don. The Church of St Peter contains a twelfth-century chancel arch and Norman aisle arcades, plus a Norman coped tomb-chest, carved with various figures.

At the main road turn right up the hill for half a mile to Kearsley Lane. Turn left to the stream and take the footbridge on the right. Follow the stream as it winds through the field. In the corner climb the stile and keep right, following the lower boundary of the field, until a path leads through the undergrowth to a small footbridge over the stream.

The farmland here forms part of Conisbrough Parks, formerly a large estate centred on the farm of the same name.

Walk up the field towards the left-hand side of the houses. Cross directly over the lane and keep ahead with the fence on the right. Climb the double stiles in the far hedge and follow the wide path through the cultivated willow thickets.

The white willow is native to Britain with silvery grey leaves that make it very distinctive from a distance. Willow bark infusions were used by herbalists to remedy chills and rheumatic pain. It was found to contain the chemical salicylic acid used to create the drug known as aspirin.

After about half a mile, the path veers to the right at a marker post. Keep straight ahead to a stile that

The headless man, Conisbrough.

29

leads out onto Park Lane, a farm track and public bridleway. Turn left.

This section of the walk also coincides with the Danum Trail, encountered earlier.

Follow the lane through the centre of Conisbrough Lodge Farm. Continue ahead at the first junction, keeping between the thick hawthorn hedges until reaching a footpath sign. At this point turn left over the stile.

Over to the left is the small hamlet of Clifton (farmstead near a bank) from where there are panoramic views over to the Pennines in the west.

Follow the wide path towards the noisy motorway, crossing a narrow bridge over the dismantled railway. Head out into the field and aim for a marker post at the right-hand edge of a clump of small trees. Having passed the trees, walk through the gateposts beyond, and then veer right to follow a ditch to the stile below the motorway embankment. Turn left and walk up the track to the underpass.

In the spring there are lots of 'woolly bear' caterpillars in this area, which eventually metamorphose into the garden tiger butterfly.

Go under the M18 and turn left over the stile. Turn right immediately before the second stile and then head up the hill beside the ditch. Where the ditch turns to the right, climb the stile ahead, and continue up the path into the village, walking up someone's drive for the last few metres.

The etymology of Micklebring is unclear, although the Anglo-Saxon for 'large' is mickle, and so could indicate a large farmstead or field system.

Turn left along Greaves Sike Lane and then right at the fork along Micklebring Lane. After one mile, the lane reaches Braithwell, passing the old manor house and the church of St James on the left.

The church of St James has an interesting Norman doorway with tympanum – the space between the door lintel and the arch above. Inside is a kneeling Elizabethan figure.

At the main road (B6376) turn right.

> *Ahead is the Butchers' Arms in the centre of Braithwell (at the broad spring) beyond which is an ancient village cross. Erected about 1191, restored in 1887, the Jubilee Year of Victoria.*

After a very short distance turn left down Austwood Lane.

> *After about 100 metres, a lane on the right leads down to the earth banks of a now long since disappeared moated hall.*

Just before the end of Austwood Lane, turn right up a signed 'byway' called Top Lane. The track follows the bottom of an embankment on the left, behind which are the massive workings of Holme Hall Quarries. Where the banking ends abruptly, turn right and follow the path along an old field boundary to the farm. At the farm, turn left and follow the lane to the road beside Lambcote Grange.

Lambcote Grange is dated 1745, with the initials 'GP'.

At the road, turn left up Grange Lane and then left again down Stainton Lane, back to the Three Tuns.

The Richard I cross, Braithwell, inscribed:
The cross was erected to commemorate The freeing from bondage of King Richard I, c.1191. Restored in the Coronation Year of Her Majesty Queen Elizabeth II 1953.

Burstwick Castle, Fort Paull Battery and Paull Holme Tower

21.5 km/13.5 miles

Explorer 292 *Withernsea and Spurn Head;*
Explorer 284 *Grimsby, Cleethorpes and Immingham*

Start from the Crooked Billet in Ryehill

*Ryehill (hill where rye is grown) is a small farming
community sited on an area of (slightly) higher ground
amid the reclaimed marshes of the Humber. A 'billet' is a
piece of wood cut to a proper length for fuel.*

Walk down Pit Lane to the telephone box on Marsh Lane. Turn left
briefly and then right, and follow the lane to the main road (A1033).
Cross straight over and follow the path directly across the large field,
as indicated by a wooden footpath sign, to a corresponding sign on
Hariff Lane.

> *In removing hedgerows, farmers are destroying the habitats of
> some birds. However, others thrive in these vast fields, like the
> curlew and lapwing, while hare also seem to enjoy these wide,
> open spaces.*

Turn left and follow the road for a short distance to where the old
railway crosses the road. Turn left.

> *This was once the Hull & Withernsea branch of the North-
> Eastern Railway, and sections of the track are still visible in the
> gravel beside the road. In 1963, the Conservative government
> commissioned a certain Mr Beeching to look into the state of
> Britain's railways. What a lot of people don't know is that, prior*

Stormy skies, Ryehill.

Coastal Walks in Yorkshire

to his report, the Tories had already closed thousands of miles of uneconomic lines, and when Harold Wilson won the 1964 general election, the Labour Party closed thousands more miles, despite Wilson's pre-election pledge to 'halt the main programme of railway closures'.

Follow the wooded cinder track all the way to Glebe Farm on Station Road.

Just before the road the path heads between overgrown brick platforms of the now converted station buildings. The term 'glebe' denotes land assigned to the priest or vicar of a parish as part of his entitlement, i.e. he was not paid much and so was given land to farm.

Turn right up Station Road to Burstwick. In the village, turn left at the junction with the main road, and then keep ahead past the war memorial at the end of Pinfold Lane.

Burstwick derives from 'dwelling' wic of a Scandinavian (Viking!) man called Bursti. Pinfold Lane indicates the site of a medieval pinfold where farm animals that had strayed during the day were kept until collected by their owners.

Follow the road all the way out of the village passing the side road to the church.

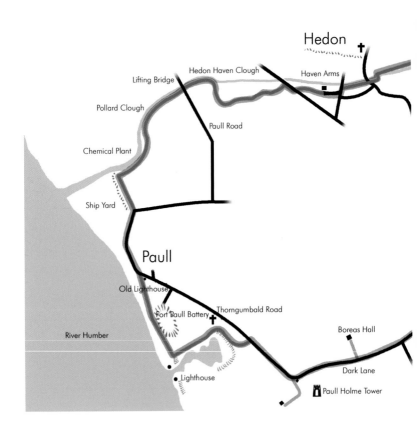

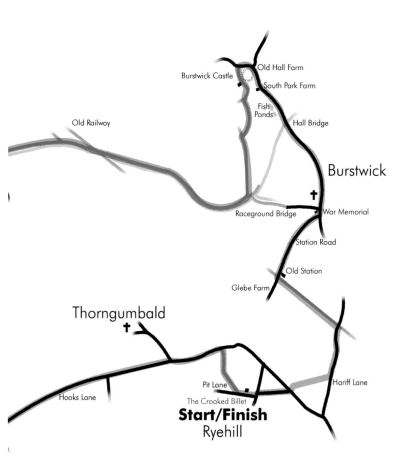

Old Hall Farm

Burstwick Castle

South Park Farm

Fish Ponds

Old Railway

Hall Bridge

Burstwick

Raceground Bridge

War Memorial

Station Road

Old Station

Glebe Farm

Thorngumbald

Hariff Lane

Pit Lane

Hooks Lane

The Crooked Billet

Start/Finish
Ryehill

The site of Burstwick Castle.

All Saints Church dates from the thirteenth and fourteenth centuries, and contains a painting of the execution of Charles I in the north arcade, placed there in 1676.

Continue up the road past the entrance to South Park Farm and left around Old Hall Farm. As the road drops and bends to the right, climb over the stile on the left. Walk up the field with Old Hall Farm now on the left, following the hedge around to the right. Climb the stile and follow the footpath sign to another stile.

This is the site of Burstwick Castle, although all that remains today are the ditch and earthen mound. Despite being a royal residence, the buildings were largely of timber, and included two chapels, a hall and chambers. The moat was added to the existing house in 1291. Burstwick Castle was once the seat of Holderness government and used as a base by Edward I and Edward III for their campaigns against the Scots in the late thirteenth and early fourteenth centuries. Indeed, Robert the Bruce's queen, Elizabeth, Countess of Carrick, was imprisoned here from 1306 to 1308, and many directions were laid down to ensure she had a comfortable stay, including servants and three greyhounds 'for her diversion in the warren and parks'.

Turn left and walk over on to the top of the mound, as indicted by the direction of the footpath arrow, aiming for a wide field gate on the right at the end of the moat.

Down to the left, the moat that would have surrounded the motte is still visible. The castle was built by William de Gros, on a slight mound amid the marshy, undrained land of Holderness. The house passed to the Albermarle family, one of whom was created Earl of Yorkshire for his prowess at the Battle of the Standard (see walk 9). The stone castle was reported as partially intact in 1782, although another report stated that, 'the old castle of the earls of Albermarle was destroyed at South Park in 1783 and the material used to mend the roads'.

Go through the gate and cross the farm lane. Take the gate to the left of the outermost building and follow the left-hand side of this building round to the back, with a pond on the left.

The medieval fishponds originally related to the castle, and then to the Old Hall, now a farm, and would have provided fresh fish for the families who lived there.

At the back of the building, climb the wooden 'stile' at the top end of the fence on the right. [This path is a local diversion and is not as shown on the OS map.] Follow the farm buildings around to the left until reaching the track. Turn left and follow the track as it turns to the left.

The small patches of woodland are home to a local population of roe deer, which are tempted out onto these flat arable 'prairies' seeking food. Modern agricultural machinery makes farming small fields uneconomical and so many miles of hedgerows have been removed to create vast fields where such technological advances can be best put to use. The roe deer is the smaller of the two native British deer and is recognised by its small antlers and a white rump.

Follow the track all the way to Burstwick Drain, and then turn right towards Raceground Bridge.

This whole landscape is crossed with such drainage dykes. They were constructed over the centuries to make the surrounding flat marshy land viable for arable farming. The dyke is filled with tall reeds, making an ideal home for reed warblers and moorhen.

Do not cross the bridge, but follow the dyke around the edge of what is now one huge arable field, keeping the dyke or drain on the left.

The rough habitat along the edge of the dyke makes a perfect home for a variety of wildlife. The striped shells of the grove snail camouflage it from predatory birds like thrushes, and this is used to demonstrate the survival of the fittest in evolution, as the least well camouflaged are easily seen and eaten.

Follow the dyke all the way to where it rejoins the old railway line. Climb up and over the line to rejoin the path beside the dyke once more.

The branch lines to Hornsea and Withernsea from Hull were both closed in 1964, one week before the General Election. As they were only really busy during the summer season it was felt that the local bus companies could satisfy demand. However, very little thought was given to the year-round commuters who depended upon this service. The local MPs kept their seats, having ensured that the lines did not close until after the 1964 summer season.

Misty lane near Hedon.

Follow the signed path through a gate and into a field with the dyke on the left. At the end of the field go through another gate and continue to follow the dike around to the left.

This walk takes place in the East Riding of Yorkshire. 'Riding' comes from the Scandinavian thrithing to mean a third, and hence there being only three Ridings in Yorkshire – East, North and West. 'South' Yorkshire is a modern administrative creation.

Follow this path between dyke and garden fences all the way long into Hedon until a small footbridge leads over the dyke.

> *Hedon (hill where heather grows) is a small town that was once a thriving seaport, although John Leland noted its decline in the mid-sixteenth century, when he said that Hedon 'used to be a fine harbour town. It stands more than a mile inland up a creek of the River Humber. Near the town this salt-water creek divides and encircles it, so that ships used to berth around the town. But now . . . some of the places where the ships berthed can be clearly seen to be overgrown with rushes and reeds. The harbour had very badly declined.'*

Once on the other side of the dyke turn sharp right and follow the dyke along the other bank. At the road, cross over and follow the path along to the next road.

> *Hedon was an important port for the export of wool, the source of much of the country's medieval wealth. As such it would have been protected although Leland also commented that, 'near [the] churchyard may be seen evidence of the site of a former tower or castle, built for the town's defence.' No trace of the castle exists today, although traces of the towns' defences do remain. The paish church of St Augustine is one of the five largest churches in the East Riding, and contains a fourteenth-century decorated font in perfect original condition.*

At the road, turn left and then right, as indicated by a footpath sign just before the old bridge. Follow the wide neat grass path with a high privet hedge on the right and continue past the Haven Arms.

> *A plaque over the door reads:*

Haven Arms
Hedon Corporation, November 25th 1825
George Sawyer, Mayor
Richard Iveson, James Matthews, Bailiffs

Continue to follow the wide grass track to the road (A1033 Hedon bypass). Go through the gate onto the road and turn right. After a few metres, cross the road and take the path indicated by the sign. Follow the signs along the path as it winds its way towards the towering chemical plant beside the River Humber. After a short distance the path climbs onto a narrow embankment that follows the line of a dried up dyke on the right.

In Edward III's time Hedon 'attracted many good ships and rich merchants, [but] now there are only a few small boats, and no merchants of any standing. Its downfall has been the diverting and sanding up of the harbour channel.' So wrote John Leland in 1540, and it is hard to imagine ships of any size sailing into Hedon today.

After about half a mile the path swings round to the right to join the side of Hedon Haven Clough. Follow this wide dyke to Paull Road at Lifting Bridge. Go straight across the road and take the track out towards the estuary with the dyke still on the right and the chemical plant beyond that.

The current Salt End sea defences were built between 1995–97, the latest of many efforts over the centuries of trying to reclaim land from the sea. The need for such a flood defence wall is well documented. When author and commentator Daniel Defoe toured Great Britain in 1724–26, he too passed through Hedon, commenting that 'at Hedon ... the sea encroaches upon the land on all that shore, and that there are many large fields quite eaten up; that several towns were formerly known to be there, which are now lost; from whence they may suppose, that as the sea by encroachment had damnified their harbour, so if it grows upon them a little more they shall stand open to the sea and so need no harbour at all.'

Climb the earth embankment at the floodgates and follow the sea wall all the way round to the village of Paull, taking in the wonderful views up the estuary towards Hull and the Humber Bridge.

When opened by Queen Elizabeth II on 17 July 1981, the Humber Bridge was the longest suspension bridge in the world (1,410 metres/4,626 feet). Today, it is currently in third place, having been superseded by both the Akashi-Kaiko in Japan (1,990 metres/6,529 feet), and the Great Belt in Denmark (1,624 metres/5,328 feet).

Drop down onto the road beside the small shipyard and turn right into the village.

Paull is a quaint old former fishing village, with three pubs along its short Main Street, the Royal Oak, the Humber Tavern and the Crown. The name 'Paull' comes from pagele *meaning 'a place where a stake or pale marks a landing-place'. Pale comes from the Latin* palus, *'a stake', and describes a long thin board, pointed at the top, used for fencing. The idiom 'beyond the pale' literally means to go into the untamed wild area beyond the fence, i.e. to an area beyond the norm, or outside the bounds of acceptable behaviour.*

At Town End Road, go straight on alongside the estuary, past the old white lighthouse and the terrace of coastguard cottages.

'This lighthouse was built in 1836 by the Trinity House of Kingston-upon-Hull. William Collison, George Hall, wardens.' Hull has long been an important fishing port. In the seventeenth and eighteenth centuries the whaling fleet would sail up the Humber en route *for Greenland, and a century later, it was the turn of the vast trawler fleet to head north into the icy fishing grounds off Iceland.*

Hull docks from Paull lighthouse.

The busy River Humber.

Follow the sea wall past the cottages and then climb a couple of steps onto the top of the embankment, with the estuary on the immediate right.

Across the estuary can be seen the industrial port of Immingham, whilst back to the north the glistening P&O ferries that sail the North Sea to Zeebrugge and Rotterdam can be seen on their berths in King George's Dock. The Humber is 2km wide at this point. It drains 20 per cent of England's land area, and is the largest outflow of fresh water from England into the North Sea.

Walk past the Old Coastguard Station, and keep beside the estuary as the path leads beside a football pitch and a car park from where fishermen try their luck at catching whiting in the tidal waters.

The coastguard station was formerly High Paull manor house, with commanding views over the river. Villagers once made a living from fishing and shrimping, but now only eel are caught commercially – to satisfy Londoners cravings for jellied eels. Paull once had eleven shrimp boats.

Continue ahead along the estuary, until a path leads up the slight hillside on the left. Hidden behind the trees at this point is Fort Paull Battery.

The site of this eighteenth-century artillery fort was first used as a defensive position by Henry VIII in 1542. At subsequent times of war it has seen further strengthening and rebuilding, particularly during the reign of Elizabeth I, and during the English Civil War, the Napoleonic Wars and the Crimean War. The present buildings were erected in 1861–64 before being remodelled once more in 1894. During World War Two, it is rumoured that some of the Crown Jewels were stored here for safekeeping. Today, it is a military museum and from the path it is possible to see the outer defence 'glacis' or embankment and ditches, plus several small underground gun emplacements.

Having passed the fort, continue ahead to the first of two lighthouses.

The old white lighthouse in Paull was superseded in the 1890s, when these two new lights were erected at the mouth of Thorngumbald Clough.

Just before the first lighthouse turn left and take the wide lane to the road, coming out beside the church. Turn right.

The Church of St Andrew and St Mary was built on high ground just outside the village in order to avoid flood damage. In 1880, while restoration was being carried out, traces of the damage inflicted by parliamentarian guns in 1642 were found, when the Royalist garrison in Fort Paull was being bombarded. The stone and carved oak pulpit dates from 1879, as do the choir stalls, but the east window is from a thirteenth-century building.

Walk down the road passing a large tidal marsh behind high flood defences on the right.

Fort Paull battery.

The Humber estuary is of international importance as a breeding and feeding ground for many species of birds. Depending upon time of year, a variety of birds can be seen including oystercatcher, dunlin, curlew, mute swan, redshank, turnstone and a variety of ducks and geese, including shelduck. Across fields to the left stands Newton Garth. The lord of the manor of Hedon, the Earl of Albermarle and Holderness, built a large manor here and a chantry with two priests. It was later the site of St Mary Magdalene's leper hospital with moats on three sides.

Continue ahead down the road, and follow it round to the left. (At this point a lane leads straight ahead. This is a private lane but it gives excellent views of Paull Holme Tower, which stands in a field to the left.)

Paull Holme Tower was once the fortified manor house of the Holme/Hulme family, who took their name from the area. A red brick tower is the sole remaining portion of the Great Hall, built in the fifteenth century. It stands thirty feet high, with battlements and small loophole windows. The ghost of a cow is

Paull Holme Tower.

Medieval doorway, Thorngumbald church.

reputed to haunt the tower after it leapt to its death from the roof in 1841. The present farmhouse was built in 1837 out of materials from the Old Hall.

Follow the road round to the left from where it is possible to catch glimpses of Paull Holme Tower through the hedge on the right. After a short distance there are extensive views over the fields and river Humber on the right.

Across the river in the far distance, it is possible to see Grimsby's famous landmark, the 300ft-high, Grade I Listed Dock Tower, built in 1851. It contains around one million bricks and was built to hold a reservoir that was installed to allow hydraulic pressure to open and close the ten sets of dock gates.

After a short distance the road passes a fine house called Boreas Hall, built on one of the few 'high' points in this flat area.

Boreas Hall was formerly Boar House or Bower House, and the grounds once extended to three hundred acres. It is built upon

> *a glacial moraine some fifteen metres above sea level. Moraine is the debris picked up by glaciers and then dumped in mounds or ridges once the ice melts. Much of the land in this area has been reclaimed from the river, and is covered with a deep soil with some clay, although on the higher grounds the soil is full of gravel.*

Follow the road (which is named Dark Lane and then Hooks Lane) all the way into Thorngumbald.

> *The etymology of this village is unclear. It is possibly 'the place at the thorn trees in the manor of the Gumbald family' (a Norman name), or derived from Thorn-cum-Paul, on account of its being in the parish of Paull, and now corrupted to Thorngumbald. St Mary's Church dates from c.1200 and contains two early medieval doors.*

At the junction with the A1033 turn right. Shortly after Camerton Hall, take the footpath on the right beside Hook's Garden Centre.

> *In 1785, Edward Ombler purchased the manor of Ryehill and Camerton and records show that Camerton Hall had been built by 1810. It was a typically grand Holderness farmer's house in red brick, with hipped slate roof, of three storeys high and with a symmetrical five-bay façade. The house was derelict by 1949 and was sadly demolished in the early 1970s.*

Follow the fence all the way past the greenhouses to a marker post in the trees. Cross the stream and take the stile into the field. Go diagonally across the field to a stile in the corner and continue across the next field to the opposite diagonal corner. Climb the stile into Pit Lane and turn left to walk the short distance back to the Crooked Billet.

right The village pond, Sicklinghall.

Spofforth Castle, Rougemont Fort and Harewood Castle

27.5 km/17 miles

Explorer 289 Leeds – Harrogate, Wetherby and Pontefract

Start from the Scotts Arms in Sicklinghall

Walk down Main Street through the village, passing the Church of the Immaculate Conception on the way to the village pond. Just after the pond, turn left down Stockeld Lane. About 50 metres after the last house (Ivy Cottage) turn left up some wooden steps in the hedge and over a stile into the field.

> *Sicklinghall is derived from 'a nook of land of the followers of a man called Sicel'. The personal name is Old English and the 'ing', which is very common in many English place-names, refers to the family or followers of a named person.*

Walk ahead with the hawthorn hedge on the right. Go into the corner of the field beneath three large oak trees and turn left up to the top corner of the field. Climb the stile on the right, cross over the ditch and another stile into the next field.

> *The lodge to Stockeld Park is in Sicklinghall Wood on the right, with the hall itself hidden by the trees. The house was built by James Paine between 1756 and 1763, although there are nineteenth-century additions, and a separate chapel in the grounds, remodelled in 1909.*

Walk straight ahead on the left of a wire fence to a stile. Drop down to cross a small stream and go up the bank to continue ahead as before. Pass beneath the large oak trees and follow the arrows round to the right. With the fence on the left, keep ahead as before beneath the trees.

> *There are lots of pheasants in these fields and nearby woods, bred for the shooting season. Toad Hole Beck is in the valley bottom down to the right.*

Climb the stile beside the gate and keep straight ahead towards the conifer plantation. Climb the stile on the left just before the tree and then walk round the corner of the plantation to follow the fence all the way down to the next stream. At the double gate turn left and cross the stream by stepping stones.

> *This area is dotted with small temporary plantations and not all are shown on the OS Map. The small wood on the top of the hill over the stream is Royal Oak plantation, behind which is Spofforth Hall.*

Go up the bank and through the gates into the corner of the next field. Follow the fence on the left for a short distance before heading out towards a stile beside a metal field gate. Pass through a gap in the hedge and follow the rough track that leads all the way to High Lane.

Spofforth (ford by a small plot of ground) is now clearly visible on the right. The houses in the village, which stands on the River Crimple, are built of millstone grit.

Turn right briefly and, having crossed the bridge, take the stone steps over the wall. Head off at 45° to the right, aiming for a track that passes through the old railway embankment.

This railway was another branch line that suffered as a consequence of consecutive Conservative and Labour governments attempting to address the difficult problem of an ageing and uneconomic railway system in Britain.

Go under the bridge and keep straight ahead to pass through a field gate. The path leads out onto the road beside the Castle public house. Down the road ahead is the parish church.

All Saints Church is classic example (or victim!) of the Victorians' Norman revival architecture, where medieval churches were gutted and re-built. However, some original features do remain, including late-Norman arcades and twelfth-century piers. In the graveyard stands the shaft of a ninth- or tenth-century cross, plus the grave of 'Blind Jack' Metcalfe of Knaresborough. He was one of the leading road builders of the eighteenth and nineteenth centuries despite being blind, and was a contemporary of Telford and Macadam.

Turn left and walk down Castle Street towards Spofforth Castle.

Spofforth Castle was an elaborate fortified manor house, dating from the reign of Edward II, when the Percy family were granted a licence to crenellate in 1309. The Percy family had been granted lands here by William the Conqueror after the invasion. Scottish raiding parties attacked the castle in 1368. During the Wars of the Roses, the Percys sided with the Lancastrians and, after the bloody battle of Towton, the victorious Yorkists slighted Spofforth Castle. It was rebuilt again, but destroyed by Parliamentary troops in the English Civil War in 1642. The earliest part of the present castle – the undercroft beneath the hall – dates from the thirteenth century and major alterations were made in the fourteenth and fifteenth centuries.

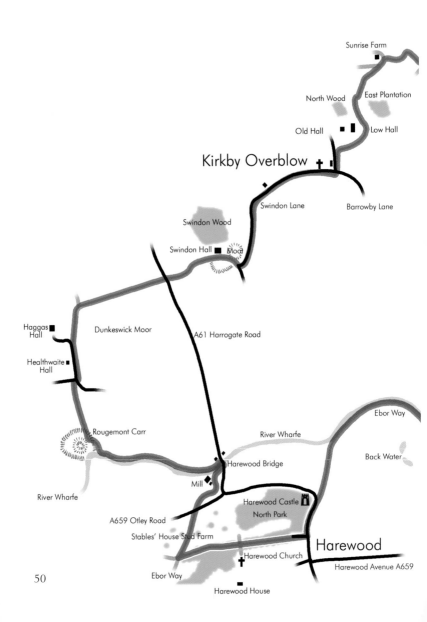

Walk 4: Spofforth, Rougemont and Harewood

Spofforth
Castle

A661

Spofforth

Lodge Farm

Cup & Ring

A661 Harrogate Road

Spofforth Hall

Royal Oak
Plantation

Toad Hole Beck

Stockeld Park House

Nursery

Sicklinghall Wood

The Scots Arms

Start/Finish

Sicklinghall

Sicklinghall Grange

Kirkby Lane

Longlands Lane

Ebor Way

Sicklinghall House

Old Wives Wood

Woodhall Hotel

River Wharfe

Spring Wood

Ox Close

River Wharfe

Carthick Wood

Woodhall Bridge

A659

Turn left up Manor Garth just before the castle.

> *September 24 is St Robert of Knaresborough's day. He lived from 1160–1218 and spent most of his life as a hermit, living for a while under a church wall in Spofforth before moving to Knaresborough.*

Follow the fence up the gravel drive and continue under the railway bridge. Turn right through a small metal gate and, after about 100 metres, turn left over Manor Bridge across Park Beck.

> *The castle would once have had extensive views in this direction but the Victorian railway embankment cuts right through the line of vision. In 1540, Leland noted that, 'The Earl of Northumberland had an excellent manor here, and a manor house with a park, but the house was badly damaged in the civil war [the Wars of the Roses] between Henry VI and Edward IV.'*

Keep ahead up the wide path through the centre of the golf course. Once over the brow of the hill, the path begins to descend towards a wooded valley. As it passes below the clubhouse, the path narrows before swinging left over the stream.

> *A common plant of wet and marshy places, or the banks of streams, is the meadowsweet with is a mass of aromatic small white flowers. It was once strewn on church floors to make the*

Spofforth Castle.

stuffy interiors smell pleasant. It is also used to flavour mead and in medicines to treat arthritis and rheumatism. The roots produce a black dye.

Go through the metal gate and head up the banking towards the telegraph pole on the right. Continue up the hill following the line of the telegraph poles with Lodge Farm over the field on the left. Follow the edge of Lodge Wood all the way to the lane.

Just up to the left, towards Lodge Farm, there is a 'cup and ring' marked rock hidden on a small hillock covered in brambles, nettles and other straggly undergrowth. The term 'cup and ring' describes a hollow chipped out in a large stone, surrounded by concentric circles. They are found mainly in northern England and Scotland, and are estimated to be around 4–5,000 years old, dating them to the Neolithic and Bronze Ages, although their precise meaning is still unknown. The boulder here (if you can find it!) has a line of seven cup-marks, two of which have rings.

Turn right and then left, up the bridleway for Kirkby Overblow, initially between high hedges. Once over the brow of the hill, take the right-hand track. At the next fork, turn right along a sparse line of trees and aim for the farm. Follow the track through the gate beside a small conifer wood and head up to the farm buildings. At the perimeter fence follow the signs round to the left. The path goes round the buildings to a stile into the lane.

This area is called Spofforth Haggs. The term hagg *refers to an enclosed woodland from which firewood was collected.*

Go straight across the lane and aim for the top left-hand corner of the field. Go through the gate and walk straight ahead to cross the lane. Follow the hedge down the next field and, after a short distance, go through the gap to the right. Continue to follow the hedge in the same direction as before, but now with the hedge on the left.

The jay is a member of the crow family, but is one of the most brightly coloured of British birds. The flash of colour can come as something of a surprise as it flits between oak trees, collecting acorns to bury in the autumn.

Cup and ring marks, near Lodge
Farm.

In the corner of the field, turn
right and up to the stile. Climb
the stile and go straight ahead
with the fence on the left. The
large chimneys of Low Hall soon
appear down to the right.

*Low Hall stands on the
outskirts of the village, hiding
the original old hall, a
seventeenth-century house
with five-light mullioned
windows on two floors. The obelisk gateposts stand at right-
angles to the much grander pair of Low Hall.*

Walk down the field over a stile, heading for a gated passageway over
the stream. Climb up the hill to the gate in front of the red brick farm
buildings. Go through the gate and over some stone steps in the wall
ahead. Follow the garden wall of the old hall on the right all the way
up to the road. Turn left.

*The name Kirkby Overblow alludes to past industrial times
when ore blowing (or smelting) was common throughout this
region. The prefix 'kirkby' denotes a village, from the
Scandinavian '-by', with a church, 'kirk'.*

Walk down through the village and, at the junction, turn right past
the church.

*St Helen's Church dates mainly to 1780, but has extensive
Victorian 'improvements' from 1872. However, it does contain
a blocked doorway, of possible Saxon origin. Approximately 100
metres beyond the church is St Helen's Well set into a recess at
the end of a walled passage. It has been suggested that the
church site and the well may have been linked in pagan times.
Many sacred springs were probably the focus of initial
settlement and soon became associated with first pagan, and*

then Christian rites. Many churches are built over sacred wells.

Walk down Swindon Lane passing Birdwell Farm.

Opposite Birdwell House lies Bird Well, where water runs from the spring into a large stone trough. On the hillside behind the farm, lies Wareholes Well, another holy well. The large stones that once paved its vicinity have since been removed making it very difficult to locate.

Where the road turns sharply to the left, go through the gate on the right and walk up the bridleway to Swindon Hall.

The imposing gates to Swindon Hall Farm.

To the right of the hall are a series of moated earthworks, indicating the site of an earlier house.

Take the field gate on the left that leads past the ornate gates at the front of the hall.

Continue past the farm buildings and turn left at the fence.

There is an enclosure earthwork clearly visible on the left in this field.

Go through the gate and walk down the hill to the stream. Cross the bridge over Keswick Beck and walk up the field, aiming slightly to the right, to an iron gate on the main road (A61 Harrogate Road). Cross straight over and walk up the bridleway opposite. At the top of Green Lane, turn left beneath the mobile phone mast and walk all the way down to the junction.

The red kite was once one of our most widespread birds of prey. Sadly, by the late 1800s the last kites had disappeared from Yorkshire and only a handful of pairs managed to survive in Wales. A national re-introduction programme began in 1989, with young birds being released in the north of Scotland and

The banks and ditches of Rougemont Fort.

southern England. In the summer of 1999, Yorkshire's re-introduction programme began when 21 young kites were released on the Harewood Estate near Leeds.

At the junction turn right briefly, signed 'Weeton ½ mile', and then turn left just beyond the house. Follow the unenclosed track all the way down to the wood, Rougemont Carr. Walk straight ahead into the trees and follow the path round to the left. At the boundary wall turn right and follow it down towards the river.

The wood covers the site of Rougemont Castle ringworks and bailey, with associated fishponds and outworks. This was once the stronghold of the Norman lord of the area, until a successor built a new castle overlooking the river from the high escarpment on the opposite bank. Rougemont is a multivallate fort, having more than one bank and ditch and often with complex entrances, although these are well hidden by mature woods and dense undergrowth. As one approaches the river the outer ditch and bank can be clearly seen. In winter it is far easier to see the inner banks and ditches through the trees as there is far less undergrowth.

The path leads through a gap in the wall to the left and then turns right down to the River Wharfe. At this point turn left, and follow the high bank for about 100 metres to where a narrow path drops further down the bank past a marker post. Follow this winding path as it meanders its way along beside the river.

The Harewood Estate has placed great emphasis on the creation of new habitat for game and has produced some notable successes. The buzzard, peregrine falcon and merlin can be seen, and a recent initiative with English Nature and the RSPB has seen the re-introduction of the red kite to this area, for the first time in over 100 years. They are now a relatively common sight, and are easily distinguishable by a long, deep-forked chestnut tail and narrow, strongly angled wings, with red/brown upper parts and dark rufous underneath.

After a few hundred metres the path climbs back up the bank on the left. Turn right over a stile and head out into the large field. Follow the River Wharfe to the bridge. Go up the bank on the right, over a stile and then through a gate to the road.

The Wharfe is home to many river birds, including moorhen, heron, mallard, pochard, dipper and merganser.

Turn right over the bridge and then immediately right again through a narrow gap in the wall. Walk ahead through Harewood Bridge sawmills and following the signs to a small wooden gate beside some tall metal railings.

A weir was built in the river to allow water to be drawn off to power the mills that once stood on the banks. Today, a sawmill still operates here although it is no longer water powered.

Cross the lane and go over the wooden stile on the left. Follow the path round the garden to the back of the house. Turn left at the hedge and then right. Walk all the way past the buildings to the small stream, Stank Beck, which leads into the tapering corner of the field where a stile leads out into the road. Turn right along the A659 Otley Road to a gate in the high wall on the far side. Follow the track all the way up the hill.

This is part of the Harewood House Estate, home of the Queen's cousin, David Lascelles, the 7th Earl of Harewood, and his wife Diane. The Earl's estate manages the countryside surrounding Harewood House and has a nationally recognised conservation programme. Particular emphasis is placed on the restoration of historic buildings ranging from Home Farm to

Red deer, Harewood Estate.

Harewood Castle.

> *Harewood Castle, as well as the protection and development of wildlife habitats and the maintenance of Listed parkland.*

At the top of the hill turn left and continue along the crest of the hill beneath mighty oak and beech trees. This path climbs for a short distance before levelling off, giving commanding views over the Wharfe valley.

> *Harewood House, through the trees on the right, is a fine example of the grand English country house. It was built by Edwin Lascelles about 1760, to designs by architect John Larr of York. The interior was designed by Robert Adam and contains furniture by Thomas Chippendale. It was remodelled and restored in 1929–39, and contains art by Turner, Reynolds Titian and Veronese, together with porcelain and lavish furnishings.*

The path continues through the deer park along the top of the wooded ridge, crossing a track that leads down to Harewood church on the right. Go straight on.

> *The original pre-Norman church was rebuilt in the early fifteenth century, c.1410, for the grand-daughters of William Aldburgh and was subsequently remodelled during the eighteenth and nineteenth centuries. It houses six fine alabaster*

tomb carvings, memorials to the fifteenth- and sixteenth-century earls of Harewood.

Follow the wide lane all the way to where it reaches the village of Harewood between two Georgian 'bookend' houses.

After the Norman Conquest the land around Harewood was given to Robert de Romelli, who built his fort at Rougemont. The medieval castle was built in the twelfth century but abandoned in the mid-seventeenth century. In 1738, the estate was bought by Henry Lascelles, whose family had made its money principally on the backs of slaves on their sugar plantations in Barbados. This fortune enabled the present Palladian mansion to be built by Edwin Lascelles in the middle of the eighteenth century. When the house was built, the village of Harewood was moved and the current estate village erected in its place.

Turn left down the A61, Harrogate Road.

Over the wall in the woods on the left just before the bend are the remains of Harewood Castle. This strongly fortified manor house was built c.1365 by Sir William de Aldburgh on a rectangular plan, possibly as a pele tower which was later developed. The licence to crenellate was granted to Sir William in 1366 by Edward III, although by the mid-seventeenth century it seems to have been abandoned and rapidly became a ruin. Much of the stone was re-used for buildings in the village, including many fine Georgian houses. The castle has recently undergone structural consolidation and is now open to the public by prearranged guided tours only, via the Harewood House Trust. 'Harewood' means literally that, a wood frequented by hares, or possibly 'the grey wood'.

Just before the bend, cross to the right-hand side of the road, and take the lane marked with an 'Ebor Way' sign.

The Ebor Way runs for 112 km/70 miles between Helmsley and Ilkley. Developed in the 1970s, it is a low-lying walk that connects the Cleveland Way to the Dales Way passing through the attractive countryside of the Vale of York. It takes its name from the Latin for York, Eboracum, through which it passes. This walk will now follow the Ebor Way to Sicklinghall House.

Follow the track, Fitts Lane, as it descends the hill all the way down to the banks of the Wharfe with The Fitts on the right. Turn right along the riverbank as it meanders down the wide valley.

The Fitts is a field name meaning 'riverside meadow-land'. Canada geese, grey lag geese and mallard can be seen on the river, as can moorhen, heron, coot and kingfisher. The Harewood Estate is responsible for managing approximately 4,000 acres of West Yorkshire on which a multitude of activities take place.

Follow the river along the flood bank all the way to Carthick Wood, climbing a couple of stiles on the way. Climb the stile into the wood and follow the winding path through the riverside wood until it leaves via the back of the wood into a field. Turn left here and follow the edge of the wood along to the river once more.

The field on the right is huge, many hedges having been removed, and it is easy to see where the river once flowed across this wide flood plain. The previous banks of the river are now high and dry, whilst Back Water is one of several ponds (or ox-bow lakes) stranded by the receding waters.

Once in the corner of the field take the path into the wood at the marker post. Follow the path to the left and then up a leafy sunken lane for a very short distance. Climb up the bank on the left into the field and follow the path all the way up the steep bank between two mighty oak trees. Turn left above a line of holly trees and follow the hedge all the way up to a fence and then on to the main road, A659. This is a very busy road. Turn left and walk for ½ mile to a left-hand turn, down the track signposted to Woodall and Sicklinghall.

Bridleways are tracks that one is traditionally allowed to lead or ride bridled horses down, as opposed to footpaths down which one can only walk.

Follow this wide bridleway, passing through two gates on the way down to the river. At the bottom of the hill follow the path round to

The River Wharfe near Woodhall.

the right and then across the wide footbridge over the Wharfe.

This is a metal girder bridge, painted green, with a wide wooden walkway. A plate reads 'Joseph Whitham & Sons, Leeds, 1868'. Flood debris high in the trees indicates that this path is severely flooded from time to time.

Follow the path over the flood plain, and then up the hill towards Woodall Hotel, with Spring Wood on the left and Old Wives Wood up the hill ahead.

The field on the immediate right is called Lawn Reign, reign deriving from rein, *the Scandinavian for 'boundary strip'.*

Walk up past the high wall of the kitchen garden of Woodhall House and then round the top corner to the right. Keep ahead through the gate into the wood and follow this track all way the past the front of the houses to a metalled lane. Turn left and follow this lane left and then right to the back of the hotel.

Wood Hall is a late Georgian house, now an hotel, of seven bays and a first floor portico of Tuscan columns.

Just before the car park, turn left down a muddy bridleway that leads over a wide stone bridge in the woods. Continue ahead up the hill and, after the houses, keep straight ahead down Longlands Lane all the way back into Sicklinghall. At the main road turn left up the hill to the Scotts Arms.

right The path from Kirklington.

Snape Castle and Marmion Tower

24.5 km/15 miles

Explorer 302 *Northallerton and Thirsk*, Explorer 298
Nidderdale, Fountains Abbey and Ripon

Start from the Black Horse in Kirklington

*Kirklington is the 'estate or settlement of the family of an
Anglo-Saxon called Cyrtla'.*

From the inn, walk directly across the top of the village green, to
where a 'no through road' drops down towards the Hall. Take the
right-hand fork into the farmyard and keep right after the buildings.
The track turns right through a gate beside a stream. Walk up the track
for a short distance to where it enters a large field.

*The old moated hall is the only surviving remnant of the lost
medieval village of Yarnwick that once occupied this area.*

Cross this field slightly to the left, aiming up the bank to where a stile

stands to the right of a solitary tree. Walk along the banking past the tree with fence on the right.

There is a holy well here called Lady Well, which may have been associated with the village. The spring head has been dug out and a brick-lined reservoir built to hold the water.

After a couple of hundred metres an arrow on a fence post indicates where the path begins to veer down the bank on the left away from the fence.

The earth mounds in these fields indicate where the lost medieval village of Yarnwick once stood.

Aim towards the far end of the fence down the bank on the left. Pass the corner of the fence and go through the wide gate marked with arrows. Turn right and follow the fence along to another gate. Keep going on the same line, following a hedgeless boundary between two fields towards a distinctive mound. At the fence, turn right briefly, and then cut left across the next field aiming towards two tall conifer trees within the grounds of Camp Hill.

Camp Hill was once the elegant seat of a Colonel Sergeantson, and is surrounded by signs of an ancient encampment, hence its name.

Go over the stile just before these trees and walk up the short field to another stile. Turn left down the drive and follow it to the junction. Turn right towards the walled garden, with the buildings of Holme Farm on the left. Follow the lane left, and then right, round to the left of the houses, to where a high brick wall appears on the right. Follow the wall to a wide gap on the right, just before the hedged drive that leads to a house ahead.

The name 'Holme' Farm refers to a farmstead built upon a slight dry mound amid otherwise marshy land or water meadows. 'Home' Farm, on the other hand, is the name often associated with the main farm at the centre of a large country estate.

Go through the gap and follow the lane as it veers to the left between a fence on the right and the hedged garden of the house on the left, all the way into Scrogs Hill Wood. After a very short distance, leave the wood on the left and turn right to a stile. Follow the edge of the wood all the way round to a wide gate in the narrow end of the field.

> *Land or field measurements are often in acres. One square mile = 640 acres; one acre = 4 roods; one rood = 40 square poles; one square pole = 30 square yards, and one square yard = 9 square feet.*

At this point turn left over a stile in the hedge. Follow the hedge along the right-hand side of the field to another stile. Keep ahead. Beneath a large tree turn right, and follow the hedge to another stile in the corner of the field. Cross this large field diagonally to the bottom left-hand corner. Go through the red gate and turn right, down the lane to the road. Turn left and walk the short distance into Carthorpe.

> *Carthorpe (farmstead of a Scandinavian man called Kari) is a small, picturesque hamlet with a manor house of c.1700.*

Keep ahead on the main through road through this small village and, after the crossroads, follow it round to the right. Keep on the pavement and follow the road all the way into Burneston.

The Mansion, Camp Hill.

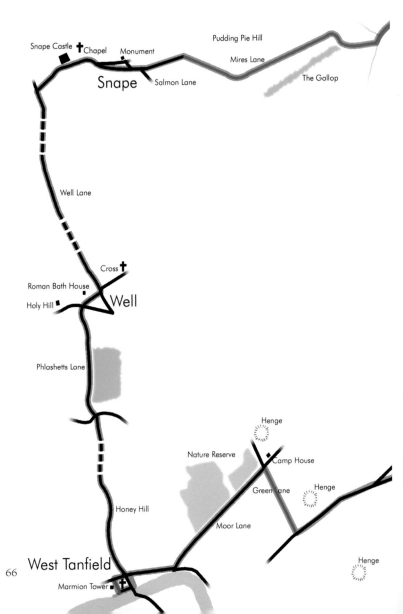

Old Hall Hill

School

Burneston

Almshouses

✝

Carthorpe

Scrogs Hill

Camp Hill

Mediaeval Village
of Yarnwick

The Hall

Moat

Start/Finish

The Black Horse

Kirklington

✝

Thornborough

Upsland Farm

Lime Lane

Moat

B6267

Almshouses, Burneston.

On the main street through Burneston (farmstead of a Scandinavian man called Bryningr) are a series of almshouses for 'five poor parishioners, aged sixty years before their admission', plus a free grammar school, founded by one of the ancestors of the present Lord Rokeby, in 1680.

Walk past the ancient Church of St Lambert and the Woodman Inn, and then turn left at the footpath sign, just before the modern school.

Sections of St Lambert's date from 1402, although the most noteworthy part of the interior are the pews, which have an inscription saying that Thomas Robinson gave £50 in 1627 to have them made. In the churchyard is St Lambert's Holy Well, a shallow artesian type, today covered with a stone slab.

Just before the school turn left down the drive of a house called Backacre and go through the large wooden gate. This may look like someone's drive but it is also a public footpath. Keep ahead past the stables and through two red metal gates to come out into a large tapering field. Walk ahead to follow the stream to the end of the field, and then walk round the circular pond on the right to a track beyond the building. Turn left and pass through the gate.

The hill on the right is Old Hall Hill, implying that an old manor house once stood here, looking out over the village.

Keep ahead down this leafy lane until a stile leads out into the field. Keeping the hedge and stream on the immediate left, cross the next three fields using the wooden footbridges to cross small dykes.

The number of dykes in this area indicates that this was once very marshy land that has long since been drained. Indeed, the area is called Snape Mires.

After crossing the second bridge, go through a gate and then turn right, to follow a line of trees round to the head of a long thin wood called the Gallop. At the wood turn right over a narrow wooden bridge to come out into a large field. Aim straight out to the solitary tree, and turn left to follow the line of an old field boundary towards a gate. Go over the stile beside the gate and follow this lane, Mires Lane, all the way into Snape.

Snape comes from the Old English snep *meaning 'boggy land'. When the castle was built the site was so boggy that oak piles in triple rows, 2½ feet in length, had to be driven into the ground to make firm foundations. These were rediscovered at the beginning of the last century when drains were being dug.*

At the village the lane turns right and then left to come out onto the road. Walk ahead at the junction into the village and continue up beside the stream that divides the village green.

On the right is the Castle Arms Inn, built in the early eighteenth century and now Grade II Listed. The pub was once a farm and included a cowbyre, piggery and foldyard, which enabled the wintering of more cattle than previously. The pig-feeding chute is still visible.

Follow the stream all the way through the centre of the village, passing the Millennium Stone and the Milbank Memorial on the way.

The Milbank Memorial, Snape.

The Millennium Stone incorporates carvings, all of which relate to different facets of life in Snape today, while at the top of the village is a monument in the form of a cross, erected by grateful friends to Lady Augusta Milbank of Thorp Perrow, who died in 1874.

Follow the road over the stream and then turn left.

Ahead at the bend is a lane that leads into the Thorp Perrow Estate. The Park contains an 85-acre arboretum that is one of the finest private collections of trees and shrubs in the country, which was the creation of one man, Colonel Sir Leonard Ropner (1895–1977). It is still owned by the Ropner family.

Follow the road to Castle Farm and Snape Castle with its medieval chapel.

The Chapel of St Mary, attached to the castle, dates from the fifteenth century and contains a series of Dutch religious reliefs. As part of the renovation, John Cecil, 5th Earl of Exeter, commissioned the artist Antonio Verrio (d. 1707) to paint the chapel ceiling with a work entitled Wonder and War in Heaven *in 1688. With the chapel being used to store grain by the mid-nineteenth century, the painting soon began to deteriorate and today it is barely visible.*

Pass the castle and follow the road round to the left.

Snape Castle started life as a simple manor house for the Neville family, and was replaced by the current stone building in 1420. In 1532, John Neville, Lord Latimer, married Katharine Parr, who resided at Snape for some years. When Neville died in 1542, Katharine married Henry VIII. Through marriage the castle came to Thomas Cecil who added crenellated battlements and a romantic Gothic exterior, c.1586. In 1798, Snape passed to the Milbanks of Thorp Perrow, and they restored the house and chapel. In the 1920s, half of Snape Castle was given into private hands and the other half remains with the Thorp Perrow estate.

Walk down the avenue of large lime trees to the road and turn left down Well Lane, all the way into Well.

Down to the left at the crossroads is Well Hall, beyond which is the church. St Michael's Church was built by Sir Ralph Neville of Snape between 1320 and 1350. It is essentially a memorial to that great family, replacing an older structure mentioned in the Domesday Book of 1086. The church contains many fine memorials to the Neville and Milbank families, one of the earliest font covers in Britain and a section of Roman tessellated mosaic pavement. In the grounds stands a very tall ancient cross. St Michael's cottages beside the church were formerly a

Snape Castle.

hospital, built in 1342, also by Ralph Neville.

In the village, turn right just after the Milbank Arms, and walk up the hill past the Methodist Chapel of 1849 to a large pond at the entrance to Holly Hill.

Half way up this hill on the right are the remains of the Roman bathhouse. This was filled by water from St Michael's Well further up the road, which gave its name to the village. This neglected well is located on the left-hand (south) side of the road, 100 metres beyond the pond and entrance to Holly Hill, although a pipe now leads it under the road. A narrow gap in the wall indicates its location. Other springs add to the stream that flows down through the village, and the remains of the Roman bathhouse further illustrate the value of this source.

At the pond, turn left and keep up the hill to the next junction. Turn right. Follow this lane (Phlashetts Lane) up, and then down, to the busy B6267. Go straight over the crossroads and follow the road all the way into West Tanfield.

To emphasise the former boggy state of the land in this area, a plashet refers to a marshy piece of land. The fields surrounding West Tanfield (open field where shoots grow) are full of grey lag geese in December. Across several fields down to the left, a large copse of trees (just to the right of the village of Nosterfield) hides the first of the three famous Thornborough henges.

Turn right at the Bruce Arms and walk along to the churchyard. Turn left down the footpath beside the graveyard to the lane.

St Nicholas's Church was built in the thirteenth century but has been 'severely' restored. There are numerous monuments to the Marmion family, including an effigy of Sir John Marmion, who died in 1387.

Turn right and the Marmion Tower is a few hundred metres ahead beside the church.

The Marmion Tower is an impressive gatehouse entrance to a former manor house that sadly no longer exists. In 1530, Leland

The River Ure and Marmion Tower (to the left of the church), West Tanfield.

comments that 'the only significant architecture I saw was a fine gatehouse with towers'. The tower has no defensive works or loops, suggesting that it was built for domestic purposes. The original tower was built c.1350–1400, although it has been added to and enlarged over the centuries. In 1513, the grandmother of Katherine Parr, the last wife and queen of Henry VIII, lived here. The Marmion family later lived here, hence its name.

Having visited Marmion Tower, head back down the lane and to the Bull Inn beside Tanfield Bridge. Turn left up to the roundabout and then right along the road. After the houses, turn left up Moor Lane, signposted 'Thirsk, Nosterfield, Carthorpe and Bedale'.

The River Ure is one of the larger rivers draining off the eastern flanks of the Pennines. Its source is on Mallerstang Common, just south of Kirkby Stephen, after which it flows through one of the best known of the Yorkshire valleys, Wensleydale, before reaching West Tanfield and the Vale of York.

Keep going ahead up the road with a large former gravel pit on the left, which is now a nature reserve.

In 2001, this old quarry site was designated a local nature reserve, having been landscaped and developed over several years to create a habitat suitable for wintering, passage and particularly breeding waders and waterfowl, including redshank, shoveler, grey partridge, reed bunting, mallard, widgeon, goldeneye, tufted duck, oystercatcher, great crested grebe, curlew, garganey, whimbrel, pochard, coot, lapwing, plover, sandpiper, teal, meadow pipit, snipe, and even cormorant. In addition to the many birds, over 200 species of plants have also been recorded.

At the junction leading left, marked 'Nosterfield ½ mile', turn right down Green Lane.

To the left at this point, behind Camp House, is the first of the three Thornborough henges, hidden by trees. No one really knows why these henges were built here 5,000 years ago, but they appear to be part of a much larger sacred landscape, between the rivers Swale and Ure. This Neolithic–early Bronze Age site comprises three large henges, a definite cursus and a possible cursus, a long mortuary enclosure, nine round barrows, two double pit alignments and other archaeological features.

At the end of Green Lane, turn left up the road. After a short distance, the second of the henges is just over the fence on the left.

By lining up the first two henges it is possible to look across several fields towards the third and final henge in the distance to the right. It is thought that the three henges may have originally been covered in gypsum, which would have made them sparkle in the sunlight. They rank in importance alongside Avebury and Stonehenge.

Follow the road all the way up into Thornborough (hill where thorn trees grow). Take the right-hand fork and follow Back Lane to the footpath sign on the right, just beyond Hillside House. Go diagonally across this field to the far left-hand corner.

The Thornborough Henges are the fifth largest of their kind in the British Isles. Their size is almost identical, each around 240m in diameter, and each with a massive ditch and bank,

Stormy skies over the Thornborough henges.

interrupted by a pair of entrances and an outer ditch. They not only share the same axis, but their entrances are all aligned north-west to south-east.

At the road turn right and walk ahead for about ½ mile to a track that crosses the road. Turn left and follow the bridleway down to the stream. Go through the gate and follow the fence around to the left for a short distance before heading out towards the far right-hand corner of the field. At the road turn left.

Farmers may consider poppies to be weeds, but they have of course become the well-loved symbol of Remembrance Day having re-colonised the battlefields of the Somme after the First

World War. The seeds can lie dormant for decades in the soil before springing to life once the soil is disturbed to carpet meadows with their bright red flowers. The yellow Welsh poppy lives in poorer upland soils, and although mainly a garden flower, it is a native species that has 'escaped' once more.

Follow Lime Lane past Upsland Farm, to a pair of footpath signs on the right. Walk up the track before veering off to the right down the well-marked path across this large field. If the field has been recently ploughed or planted the path may not yet be visible. Aim to the right of the telegraph pole and then look ahead for the solitary tree.

The path here has been well marked by the responsible landowner, who has eradicated the crop along the line of the path, thus making it easier for walkers to follow the correct route and ensuring that they do not wander aimlessly over his crops. If only more landowners followed this fine example ...

Aim for the solitary tree and the footbridge beyond. In the next field follow the left-hand boundary beside the winding stream to where it is carried by an aqueduct over another stream. Go over the footbridge and keep ahead beside a wide dyke.

Hare enjoy these wide, open fields. In the spring, the males have a habit of chasing and sparring with each other, giving rise to their nickname of 'mad March hares'

Follow the embanked dyke for a short distance, and then head up the hillside away from the stream, and round to the right. Follow the top of the embankment down a long line of trees towards the churchyard.

St Michael's Church has Norman origins with much rebuilding in the thirteenth century. Worthy of mention are a Jacobean pulpit and the fourteenth-century effigies of a knight and his lady.

At the wall turn right and then turn left at the road. Follow the road, or cut through the churchyard, back to the village green in Kirklington. Walk along the road that cuts diagonally across the green, back to the starting point.

left Field path near Upsland Farm.

Skipton Castle and Barden Tower

29.5 km/18.5 miles

Explorer OL2 *Yorkshire Dales – Southern and Western areas*

Start from the Masons' Arms in Eastby

Turn left out of the pub and walk down the main street (Barden Road) through the small hamlet of Eastby.

Eastby (east farmstead) is a small moorland village overlooking the market town of Skipton. Common Anglo-Saxon place-names often end in '-ham' or '-ton' (Skipton, Bolton) while Danish or Norwegian place-names often end in '-ber' '-by' or '-thwaite'. The fact that Skipton lies in the heart of the valley and Eastby is on the moors implies that when the Scandinavians came looking for land they found the best areas already occupied by the English and so they had to make do with the upland sites.

Take the footpath on the left just after the last house and walk down a walled path. Turn right through a small wooden gate and follow the narrow tarmac path diagonally across two fields, towards the church.

This is the parish church of St Mary the Virgin, serving both Embsay and Eastby.

Turn left at the road and, just after the church, turn right through a gate in the wall. Walk out diagonally across the field to a stile in the far left-hand corner. Walk down the enclosed path over two sets of stone steps in the walls.

The houses and village of Embsay (enclosure of an Anglo-Saxon man called Embe) are on the left.

Turn half right and head across the field to a metal field gate, and then walk along the top of the school playing field. Keep straight ahead to the wall and cross directly across the lane. Veer towards a stile in the far left-hand corner of this field, and then head right, up around the fence, to another field gate. Near the buildings, begin to veer to the left to a stile that leads out onto the road. Turn left.

On the right at this point is a large millpond, while on the left is the old manor house dated 'YM 1665'.

Just beyond this house, turn right over the footbridge that crosses the millrace. Take the steps down the steep ravine and up the other side. Head straight out across the field to a large sycamore tree, behind which is a gate. In the housing estate, go right and then immediately left down Hill Top Close, to the end of the cul-de-sac.

The red campion is widespread across the country in woodlands and in shady lanes. It is very similar to the white campion, and when the two are in proximity a pink hybrid is produced. The red is a native species, but it is thought the white variety came to Britain with migrating peoples from Central Asia during the Stone Age.

A footpath leads between a beech hedge and a wooden fence to a stile. Follow the path right, and then left along the back of the houses. In the field, head towards the large barn and then turn right up

Field path behind Embsay.

Brackenley Lane, passing beneath the railway bridge and then over Eller Beck. Walk up the hill and, after about 50 metres, turn left into the field. Walk up the gentle slope with the hedge on the right.

The Yorkshire Dales have long been known for the production of wool, and there are many different varieties of sheep to be seen, including the Blackface and the Swaledale, easily recognizable by its shaggy, curly wool.

At the brow of the hill, aim for a farm gate slightly to the left. Go through and walk ahead with the field boundary now on the left. In the corner of the field climb the stile, cross over a patch of rough ground, and pass into the golf course.

Although a sign informs walkers to give way to golfers, this is not correct. As a public right of way a footpath has precedence over the golf course, which is a much later feature, having only recently been deposited on the landscape. Golfers should give way, as the footpath has the same legal rights as any public highway.

Follow the green posts in a straight line across the golf course to a stile, and then head down to cross directly over the main road. Follow the path down to the lane and turn left. Head towards a field gate, but take the stile on the right that leads into Skipton Wood.

The Woodland Trust manages Skipton Wood, and it is the Trust's millennium wish 'to celebrate, protect and save Britain's ancient woodland'. Today, the Trust has created waymarked trails through at least fourteen ancient woods across Britain. This wood has over 1,000 years of history, and the inhabitants of Skipton and Skipton Castle have long been using it as a source of food, fuel, water, power and building materials.

The path follows the top boundary wall of the wood around to the left.

There are at least seventeen different types of trees in Skipton Wood, including oak, beech, hornbeam, lime, sweet chestnut, sloe, yew and ash. There are also over 160 plants, ferns, grasses and sedges, including three different orchids.

After a couple of hundred metres, a series of steps lead down to the banks of Eller Beck. Go left over the stile and then follow the path over the head of the culverts through which Eller Beck runs under the bypass. Drop down the other side and take the path that follows the stream back into the wood.

The wood is also home to several mammals, including five species of bat, badger, fox, grey squirrel and roe deer.

Walk ahead into the wood with the stream on the right, along a terraced footpath half way up the escarpment.

Eller Beck is home to heron, dipper, kingfisher and mallard. The stream has been dammed with a weir to create Long Dam on the right, while in the centre of the wood the path passes between this and Round Dam on the left.

Cross a small bridge over the stream and continue ahead, with Eller Beck now in a deep gulley on the left, until the path leaves the wood by a small wooden gate.

The buildings here were once all mills, powered by the water of Eller Beck. The millponds were built to enable a regular flow of water to power the mills. The house on the left carries a date stone, 'Old Saw Mill c.1785'.

Follow the lane along the back of the castle into the town. Turn left down Raikes Road and then left across the river and millrace. Having passed the Castle public house, enter the churchyard through a metal gate.

Holy Trinity Church contains the decorated remains of a rood screen dated 1533. The rood screen hid the altar and cross from the congregation, rood being the Anglo-Saxon for 'cross'. The church also contains an effigy of Sir Henry Clifford who had rebuilt the castle.

Pass the front of Holy Trinity Church and come out in front of the castle. Turn right.

Skipton Castle dates from the Norman period, when Robert de Romille built a fortress on a naturally defensive cliff above the

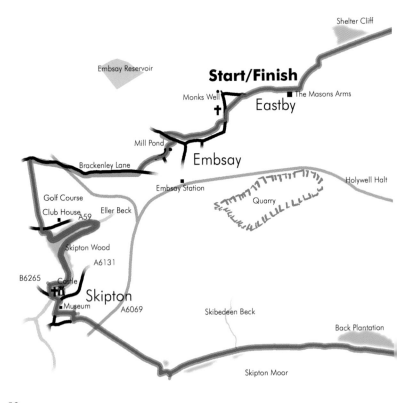

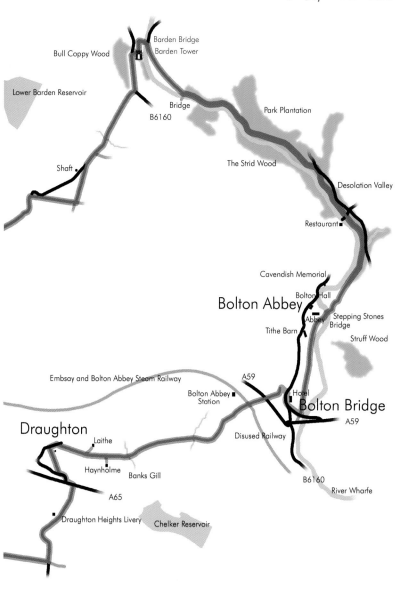

Barden Bridge
Barden Tower
Bull Coppy Wood
Lower Barden Reservoir
Bridge
B6160
Park Plantation
The Strid Wood
Shaft
Desolation Valley
Restaurant
Cavendish Memorial
Bolton Hall
Bolton Abbey
Abbey
Stepping Stones
Bridge
Tithe Barn
Struff Wood
Embsay and Bolton Abbey Steam Railway
A59
Draughton
Bolton Abbey
Station
Hotel
Bolton Bridge
A59
Laithe
Disused Railway
Haynholme
Banks Gill
A65
B6160
River Wharfe
Draughton Heights Livery
Chelker Reservoir

The gateway, Skipton Castle.

river, although very little of that original castle remains. It was strengthened and enlarged over the centuries until the Civil War, during which the royalist garrison held out for three years against parliamentarian troops. After its capture, Cromwell ordered it to be destroyed. From 1657 to 1658, Lady Anne Clifford was granted permission to repair the castle with the provision that it would no longer be capable of a serious defence. The restoration saw the round towers and walls rebuilt but with the inclusion of windows.

Walk down the main street to take the second street on the left, Otley Street. Continue ahead and turn right at the junction with Rectory Lane. Walk down Bunkers Hill and turn left along Newmarket Street. Walk ahead to the mini-roundabout and keep ahead along Newmarket Street leading to Shortbank Road. Follow this road as it begins to climb up the hill.

The old toll cottage on the left is identifiable by a room that sticks out at a right-angle into the road. This room would have a window on either side allowing the toll-bar keeper to keep his eye open for travellers, who would then be charged to enter the town. In particular, travelling merchants were charged so that local trades people would have an advantage in their own town on market day.

Climb to the top of the hill and, where the road peters out at the end of the houses, go straight on up the bridleway.

The last house on the right has an interesting display of architectural relics embedded in the walls and garden, including mock ruins, archways, gargoyles and battlements.

Follow a distinctive line of kerbstones set into the ground, as the track veers first left and then right beside a small copse of tall beech trees.

These kerbstones mark the edge of a former paved section of a medieval causeway. Cobbled and paved packhorse routes criss-cross the upland regions, and once provided vital links between small isolated industrial settlements and markets further afield. Causeways (from the Latin via calciata, *'path paved with limestone') are paved tracks, sometimes just a single line of pavestones between walls that allowed quicker and easier walking for pedestrians or pack animals.*

Where the path enters a patch of gorse follow the left-hand fork and come out beneath the cliff of an old quarry. Turn left and walk up through the wood, along a wide cobbled surface. Keep ahead over Jenny Gill and continue up through the leafy beech wood with the steep hillside dropping way to the left.

The hill on the right is Skipton Moor with a field, 'Vicar's Allotment', on the slopes, the name of which implies glebe land belonging to the local parish priest.

Eventually the path levels off and follows the contours along the hillside. Keep the wall on the left, passing a number of small woods on the right and Back Plantation on the left, until reaching a narrow road. Turn left and walk down the hill to the A65. Cross over and take the small road down towards Draughton.

Draughton is a small hamlet that has neither shop not pub. Although there is a small chapel, shops and pubs are focal

Grazing sheep, Draughton.

points of small communities where people can meet, mix and socialise, and so without them villages often appear lifeless. The official definition of a hamlet is a 'small village without a church, but in the same parish as another village or town'.

After 50 metres, climb over the wall on the right and walk down the field, aiming for some stone steps in the wall to the left of the house. Head left and then turn right along the lane. Just before Thornber Laithe, take the right-hand fork over the cattlegrid and up the hill.

A laithe is a barn for livestock or grain, often attached to a farmhouse.

Where the lane turns right to Haynholme, go straight ahead through the gate and walk down the field to cross the stream. Aim towards the telegraph pole and then follow a slight depression up the field to a gate. Go through the gate and keep ahead with the wall on the right, passing another two fields. After crossing the stream, aim for the mobile phone mast, and go through the gate. After about 20 metres, bear left down towards the trees by a stone wall.

The terminus station of the Embsay & Bolton Abbey Steam Railway is down to the left, whilst Bolton Abbey itself is clearly visible in the valley bottom ahead.

Follow the sunken green path as it descends and crosses the old railway bridge and continue down a line of old oak trees. Go through the gate and walk down the gravel path to cross directly over the main road (A59). Climb the banking and walk straight down the field. Just before the wall, turn left and cross Hambleton Beck by a neat wooden footbridge. Turn right and climb the steps over the wall into the road. Turn right and go out through a gate onto the B6160.

The hotel opposite is the Devonshire Arms Country House Hotel, as the land here is part of the Duke of Devonshire's Yorkshire estate. In September 1833, Charlotte, Emily and Anne Brontë met friends at the hotel, before moving on to visit the Abbey ruins during an excursion from their home at Haworth in West Yorkshire.

Turn right past the hotel and then left up Beamsley Lane. Just before Bolton Bridge over the River Wharfe, turn left through a stile and follow the riverside path to Bolton Abbey.

Bolton Abbey is a quaint village adjacent to Bolton Priory. Although the village is called Bolton Abbey, the monks here founded a priory in 1154 – it was never an abbey. In 1135 Alice de Romilly founded a religious house at Embsay but it moved to this site on the banks of the River Wharfe in 1154. The Priory of Augustinians, the 'black canons' surrendered to the king at the suppression in 1540, after which it became a chapel to Skipton. Much of what remains is from the twelfth century, although the tower was not begun until 1520. The Duke of

Bolton Priory.

Devonshire's house, Bolton Hall, incorporates the fourteenth century gatehouse to the priory, and other additions over the centuries.

At the priory cross the river using either the bridge or the stepping stones. Take the right fork up the steep banking into the woods, keeping to the high bank as it follows the meandering Wharfe. After a short distance the path begins to descend though the beech woods to a narrow road.

On this section of the walk the path follows a permissive path, which is also the route of the Dales Way. After about half a mile there is a fallen tree embedded with hundreds of bent coins. The Dales Way is an 84-mile long distance footpath that leads from Ilkley through the beautiful Yorkshire Dales National Park to Bowness-on-Windermere in the Lake District. Attractions en route include the riverside beauty spots of Bolton Abbey and Burnsall in Wharfedale, the upper reaches of Langstrothdale and the moors above Ribblehead (on the famous Settle to Carlisle Railway Line), as well as Dentdale, Sedbergh and the Howgill Fells.

Turn left down the road and through the ford before heading left once more back towards the river.

The River Wharfe rises on the high moors of Langstrothdale

Chase before passing through Buckden, Kettlewell and Kilnsey, after which it flows on through Grassington and Burnsall. After Bolton Abbey, the river leaves the Yorkshire Dales National Park and continues on to Ilkley and Otley to meet the River Aire in the Vale of York en route for the Humber Estuary and the North Sea.

Turn right over a stile into a field and follow the riverbank all the way through the woods to Barden Bridge, always staying on the right-hand bank.

The path goes through the 'Valley of Desolation' and Strid Wood, an SSSI conservation site. Woodland birds include coal tit, chaffinch, robin, wren, spotted woodpecker, blue tit and great tit, whilst on the river are heron, goosander, mallard, dipper and kingfisher.

Where the Posforth Bridge crosses Sheepshaw Beck, use the footbridge on the left and walk ahead into the woods. The path winds and climbs up the bank, but the river is never very far away down to the left.

At intervals there are wooden benches that allow wonderful views up and down the river, including the very rustic (and welcoming) Harrison's Ford Seat. One gives views upstream towards the Strid, whilst another is perched high above this famous geological site. The Strid is a notorious narrow section where the River Wharfe is forced into a deep, thundering channel. At its narrowest point, the

The Strid, River Wharfe.

Barden Tower.

Strid is only about two metres wide, and anyone foolish enough to try and leap across seriously risks being sucked into the swirling, dark waters. This is a very dangerous place.

Eventually the path leads out into the meadows of the flood plain. Continue to follow the riverbank past a wonderful (and somewhat unexpected) battlemented Devonshire estate bridge, where a sign indicates a path to Cony Warren up to the right.

The name 'cony warren' describes an area where rabbits were once bred, having been introduced into England in the twelfth century by the Normans. In some instances burrows were dug for the conies (from the Norman-French conis *meaning 'rabbit') and they were farmed for fur and meat.*

Follow the river all the way to the splendid three-arched Barden Bridge. Cross the bridge and walk up the road, and round to the left, to Barden Tower.

Barden Tower was built as a forest hunting lodge in the twelfth century. It is one of six hunting lodges associated with Barden Forest, and was rebuilt by Sir Henry Clifford in the late fifteenth century and by Lady Ann Clifford in 1658–59. It is claimed that Henry Clifford preferred to live here rather than in Skipton

Castle and his pastoral activities earned him the nickname of the 'Shepherd Lord'. In 1658, Lady Anne Clifford restored the building and the result is a wonderful blend of fifteenth- and seventeenth-century architecture. It is hard to tell which part belongs to which century, although a noticeable fifteenth-century fireplace has been cut in half by a seventeenth-century wall. In its heyday, the tower and courtyard were surrounded by a wall with two entrance arches, one of which still stands.

Walk up the road past the tower to the next junction. Turn right (signed to Embsay) and walk up, and then down, this road crossing Barden Beck on the way. As the road begins to climb the hill take the second footpath sign on the left. Go through the stile and take the right fork, walking up the hill to the skyline.

Much of this area is bracken moorland, famed for grouse shooting and hunting, on the Duke of Devonshire's Yorkshire country estate.

At the brow of the hill, turn right along a wide green path to a gate. Turn left over the cattle grid and follow the road all the way back to Eastby.

The moors above Wharfedale.

Helmsley Castle

26 km/16 miles

Explorer OL26 *North York Moors, Western area*

Start from the Wombwell Arms in Wass

Wass is derived from the Old Scandinavian word vath *for 'ford', in its plural form.*

From the front of the pub, walk ahead at the crossroads (west) up the dead-end lane, with the steep road up Wass Bank to the right.

> *Wass Bank climbs up the steep escarpment that marks the sudden edge of the Hambleton Hills. Not far to the north-west is the White Horse of Kilburn, etched into the hillside, and, beyond that, Sutton Bank.*

Just before the white house on the right, take the footpath on the left. Follow the wood round to the right and then go through a gate before dropping down the bank. The path leads to a stile in the fence, just

The crossroads, Wass.

Medieval floor tiles, Byland Abbey.

to the left of Abbey House Farm. Climb two other stiles on the way to the farm drive. Turn left and walk to the road in front of the abbey.

> *Byland Abbey was founded by Cistercian monks from Stocking in 1177, although the building work was not completed until the mid-thirteenth century. There are a number of unique features that make Byland Abbey one of the finest ruins in England, including the north side of the church which stands in its entirety, and an amazing number of medieval floor tiles which still lie in situ. Over the small road opposite the front of the abbey, stands the remaining arch of the original gatehouse. The grounds house a small museum of finds.*

Turn left and follow the road to the corner, but keep ahead down the track to a stile on the left. Turn right in the field and take the right-hand of two stiles in the fence. Walk past the telegraph pole and up the far bank to the road. Turn right briefly and then left over the stile into the field.

> *In the thirteenth century, a 'large round silver thing like a disc' was seen flying over Byland Abbey, which 'caused the utmost terror', according to a chronicler of the time.*

Rievaulx

✝ Ionic Temple
Rievaulx Abbey

■ Tuscan Temple
Abbot Hag Wood

Rievaulx Bridge

Site of Mediaeval
Village of Griff

Hags Wood

Hollins Wood

Whinny Bank
Wood

Bungdale Heap Slack

Deer Farm
A170

Sproxton Moor

Wass Moor

The Royalty

Abbey Bank Wood

Start/Finish

Wass ■ Wombwell Arms

Burtis Wood

Carr House

✝ Byland Abbey

Ampleforth

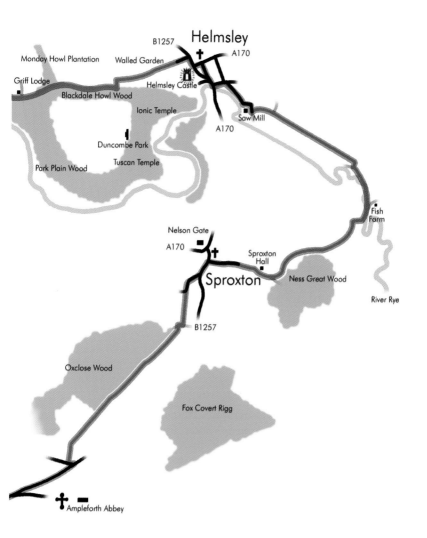

Monday Howl Plantation
Griff Lodge
Blackdale Howl Wood
Walled Garden
B1257
Helmsley
A170
Helmsley Castle
Ionic Temple
A170
Saw Mill
Duncombe Park
Tuscan Temple
Park Plain Wood
Fish Farm
Nelson Gate
A170
Sproxton Hall
Sproxton
Ness Great Wood
River Rye
B1257
Oxclose Wood
Fox Covert Rigg
Ampleforth Abbey

The path follows the contours round to the right running parallel with the road. Keep ahead through a gate and then cross Burtis Beck by a small, gated footbridge. Cross the lane and continue ahead to the wood and another stile and footbridge. Head for the telegraph pole and then drop down to the far corner of the field on the right, where a stile leads out onto the road. Turn left and walk into the village of Ampleforth.

> *Ampleforth (where sorrel* [ampre] *grows at the ford) is a small linear settlement straddling the road, famed for its abbey and college. St Hilda's Church has a Norman doorway and a Norman font. The rest dates mainly from 1868.*

Walk straight through the village passing the White Horse and the White Swan pubs, before taking the left fork up the hill, signposted 'Helmsley 4 miles'. At the top of the hill turn left and then right down the footpath just beyond Beacon House. Walk directly out across the centre of these large fields aiming for the right-hand edge of a large wood, called Salmon's Wood.

> *Ampleforth Abbey was established by Benedictines in 1803. It was initially just a house but wings were added to enlarge it, followed by the school, which is connected by a Gothic-style grange. Today, it is an impressive, modern Roman Catholic monastery and college.*

Follow the right-hand side of the wood down the hill, climbing a stile on the way. Turn left round the end of the wood and then turn right in the lane. After 50 metres, take the stile on the left and walk up the field with the fence on the left. At the hedge, climb the stile on the left and turn right to drop the short distance down to the lane. Follow the lane ahead and round to the road. Turn left.

> *St Chad's Church in Sproxton is post-Restoration, and contains plaster figures in relief based upon* The Entombment *by Michelangelo, which is housed in the National Gallery. Sproxton is the settlement* tun *of a Scandinavian man called Sprok or Sprogh, i.e Sprok's* tun.

Walk up into the small hamlet of Sproxton towards the church.

The Nelson Gate, Duncombe Park.

Down the road at this point is the Nelson Gate, or Arch, 1806, a triumphal arch with Tuscan columns and entablature, which was once one of the many grand entrances into Duncombe Park. The inscription above the gateway reads: 'To the memory of the Viscount Lord Nelson and the unparalleled gallant achievements of the Royal Navy'.

Just before the church turn right down the lane.

The tall metal pipe on the corner by the bench is an old Victorian sewer pipe that allowed 'foul air' to be released into the atmosphere without assaulting peoples' senses.

Follow the lane all the way to Sproxton Hall. Take the lane to the right of the hall and, at the next junction, take the left-hand track.

A sign here indicates that the route now coincides with the Ebor Way and that it is 2½ miles to Helmsley. The Ebor Way runs for 112 km/70 miles between Helmsley and Ilkley. Developed in the 1970s, it is a low-lying walk that connects the Cleveland Way to the Dales Way passing through the attractive countryside of the Vale of York. It takes its name from the Latin for York, Eboracum, through which it passes.

At Low Parks Farm, turn off the track before the farm entrance, and keep ahead to pass through a large wooden gate. Turn right towards

The River Rye near Helmsley.

the edge of the wood, and follow it down to a field gate at the very bottom of the field. Walk down the next field into the bottom left-hand corner and then take the gate in the thick hedge on the left. Turn right and go through another gate into the next field.

In the trees on the right is an 'ox bow lake', formed when a river's meanders meet and forge a new route downstream, leaving the former bend as a pool.

Keep this stagnant pond on the right and walk ahead down the hedge line. Where there is a large gap in this old field boundary, turn right and walk to the gated metal footbridge over the River Rye. Cross the river and turn left between the river and the fish farm. Follow the track round the bend to the right and then take the footpath through the gate on the left. Walk ahead through the undergrowth to another gate.

Cow parsley is a member of the carrot family and is a common sight down rural lanes and farm tracks across the countryside. It is a robust perennial with tall, branched stems and small white flowers, massed in flat-topped heads or umbrels. Although edible, it is related to the poisonous hemlock. It is also known as Queen Anne's lace.

Go up the banking on the right and turn left. The path gradually heads towards an old railway embankment on the right, with the river on the left. Go through the embankment, turn left and continue ahead towards Helmsley, as the path begins to veer away from the old railway.

About half a mile over fields to the right lie the remains of a Roman villa at Riccal Bridge outside the small village of Beadlam on the A170 road from Helmsley. It is accessible at any reasonable time and features winged-corridor villa walls and a hypocaust (Roman central heating system).

Continue straight ahead across a large field to a hedge that juts out into the field, using the towers of Helmsley Castle and the church as guides. Keep straight ahead with the hedge on the immediate left. Go through two gates into a lane leading to a sawmill. At the buildings turn right and follow the lane into the town. Turn left and then right at the main road (A170).

The entrance to Duncombe Park is on the immediate left at this point. Sir Charles Duncombe (ex-lord mayor of London) purchased the Helmsley Estate in 1689, and shortly thereafter he employed William Wakefield (or possibly Vanburgh) to build his baroque mansion overlooking Helmsley Castle and the valley of the River Rye. It was completed in 1713. After the First World War the house became a girls' school for 60 years until reclaimed by the Earl of Faversham, a direct descendant of Duncombe. Since 1986, Lord and Lady Faversham have undertaken extensive and sensitive restoration of the buildings and interiors, employing only the finest craftsmen to create a family home once again.

Follow the road all the way into the market square.

Red rooftops of Helmsley.

Helmsley (woodland clearing lea of an Anglo-Saxon man called Helm) is a bustling market town. It has several hostelries set around a wide square, in the middle of which stands a memorial to William, Second Lord Faversham 'erected by his tenantry in respect and gratitude, 1798–1867.' Market day is Friday, when market stalls surround the impressive memorial and the stone market cross.

Cross the square by the memorial and take the street to the left of the Tourist Information office that leads over the stream. Turn right and the entrance to the castle, with its wonderful new visitor centre, is on the left.

Helmsley Castle dates from 1186, when Robert de Roos was Lord of Helmsley. It is believed that the castle occupies the site of an earlier fortification dating back to Roman times. The impressive ruins are set within a wonderful network of high curtain walls and an immense ditch system. During the Civil War, the castle was besieged for three months, and later bought by Sir Charles Duncombe, whose family still owns it.

Helmsley Castle.

Keep ahead past All Saints Church and turn left opposite the Faversham Arms, signposted 'footpath to Rievaulx'.

All Saints Church is of thirteenth-century origin with a Norman chancel arch. It contains a small piscina in the north aisle, plus a tenth-century hogback tomb. These particular tombs are of Scandinavian origin and made in the shape of a large carved hog's back.

Walk up the road to the car park, passing a large carved rock on the left.

This is a marker stone for the start of the Cleveland Way, which runs around the North Yorkshire Moors from Helmsley before following the coast down to Filey. The Cleveland Way signs are easily identified by an acorn motif.

Keep straight ahead up the track, with a large walled garden down to the left.

Helmsley Walled Garden is a beautiful five-acre walled garden set against the spectacular backdrop of Helmsley Castle. Originally built to supply the Duncombe estate with fruit, vegetables and cut flowers, it has been extensively restored as a fully working kitchen garden, and is open to the public.

Continue up the hill until the path turns sharp left towards the wood. This path is well defined and well marked. Turn right along the top of the wood.

The wood is bounded by a fence and an ancient broken down stone wall that marks the limits to the Duncombe Park estate. Duncombe Park contains 450 acres of parkland and gardens through which run a series of walks and discovery trails. It became a National Nature Reserve in 1994 to protect the mature hardwood trees, and the animals that live and feed off them. Some of the trees are over 250 years old.

Continue ahead to where the path enters the wood, Monday Howl Plantation. Drop sharply down a series of steps and then back up the other side of a steep gulley. Go through the gates out of the wood and continue along the edge of the wood to Griff Lodge. Cross the lane

Griff Lodge, Duncombe Park.

and take the footpath across the front of the small house.

> *This wonderful Georgian gatehouse would once have guarded one of the many entrances into Duncombe Park. Gatehouses were often built in the style of the 'big' house and can offer a tantalising glimpse of the grandeur that lies beyond. Within the grounds there are 35 acres of eighteenth-century landscaped gardens that were created on a plateau, which contain vast grass terraces, woodlands, classical temples, a Yew tree walk, an Old Father Time sundial, ha-ha, 'secret garden' and an early eighteenth-century water tower. The extensive landscaped grounds include the Duncombe terrace and Rievaulx terrace, both of which contain Ionic, Tuscan and Doric temples.*

Follow the top of the beech wood once more with open fields on the right. This is Whinny Bank.

> *The earthwork mounds in the fields on the right indicate the site of the deserted medieval village of Griff (place of the deep valley or hollow). The site is a Scheduled Ancient Monument and contains well-preserved earthwork complexes. The village was probably cleared and replaced by a grange to the east of Griff Farm.*

The wide path soon re-enters the wood and slowly begins to descend, passing several old quarries on the way. At the fork keep left, to follow the path as it descends steeply to the road. At the road turn left with Abbot Hag Wood on the right and the River Rye over fields on the left.

> *The name Rievaulx is derived from 'Rye-valley', although the origins of the Celtic name 'Rye' are unknown. Like Jervaulx, the French name comes from the Cistercian monks of Clairvaulx, who colonized England in the twelfth and thirteenth centuries.*

After a short distance the road crosses Rievaulx Bridge from where a side road runs down the short distance to Rievaulx Abbey.

> *Rievaulx was the first Cistercian abbey to be founded in the north, in 1131 by Walter d'Espec. The elegant refectory is still standing amid the most complete and beautiful Cistercian ruins in England which nestle in a secluded, wooded valley where the monks could maintain a simple but harsh lifestyle. English Heritage manages the abbey, but the National Trust owns the woods on Rievaulx Terrace which contain Ionic and Tuscan temples which date from 1758, similar to those at Duncombe Park.*

Cross the bridge and continue along the road to a footpath just after the house and old barn on the left. The track swings left and then up to the right. At the fork, take the right-hand track up into the wood.

> *Perhaps the greatest influence on the landscape in this area was*

Rievaulx Abbey.

that of the monasteries and priories of a number of religious communities. The earliest foundation was via a grant of land to a group of Cistercian monks at Rievaulx, and within the next 70 years Byland Abbey had been established, together with five priories in the region.

Follow the bridleway up the hill passing through the silver birch trees, to come out onto open land. Keep the wood on the right and pass through the wooden gate. Take the left-hand fork to the next gate and continue along the sunken lane, climbing all the time up onto Scawton Moor.

This sunken lane was once probably the main route between Rievaulx and Byland Abbeys, the result of centuries of travellers between the two great religious houses. The monks were successful farmers, particularly of sheep and, as they acquired more land, they established 'granges' further and further away from the abbey. They developed large-scale moorland grazing and helped the country's economy by stimulating the rapid growth of the wool trade in the Middle Ages.

Follow the lane up Claythwaite Rigg to a set of telegraph posts and then go through the gate. Carry on towards a small clump of trees. Go through the gate and then walk up the right-hand side of the trees to another gate. Continue up the sunken lane beside Hags Gill Slack aiming for the farm through which a lane leads to the main road, A170.

At the farm, deer is bred for venison. Over to the right, the fields are full of red and fallow deer. The red deer is native to Britain, whilst the fallow deer was introduced by the Normans in the eleventh and twelfth centuries.

Turn right and then cross the main road to take the footpath opposite High Lodge. Walk ahead into the pine forest on Wass Moor, keeping ahead at the crossroads. The path soon comes out onto a forestry road. Turn left and then turn right at the road to drop down Wass Bank, back to the Wombwell Arms in Wass.

Pickering Castle
and Cropton Motte

20.5 km/13 miles

Explorer OL27 *North York Moors, Eastern area*

Start from in the Middleton Arms in Middleton

IMPORTANT NOTE: one short section of this walk,
north of Pickering, is closed on Sundays
from April to October, 9.00–17.00.

From the Middleton Arms, turn left up Church Lane Nova. Go up the
lane past the church and then turn right. Follow this lane back down
to the main road.

> *The church of St Andrew has a Saxon tower and Anglo-Danish*
> *crosses, plus stalls inside, one of which has a misericord.*
> *Misericords are hinged seats that have a carved rest underneath*
> *so that, when in the upright position, monks could rest against*
> *them to give the appearance of standing, whilst not actually*
> *sitting down.*

Turn left and then left again, towards the centre of Pickering opposite
a filling station. After about ¼ mile, turn left up Swainsea Lane. Go
up the road for a short distance and then take the footpath on the
right between the houses, with a school beyond. On the right of the
path is an earthen motte.

> *Beacon Hill is thought to be either the site of the predecessor*
> *of the current Pickering Castle, or a siegeworks, thrown up by*
> *an attacking army from which it could bombard the castle. Such*
> *a fortified mound would have provided a strategic position for*
> *a body of armed men to watch the castle garrison, with the aim*
> *of catching it during an unguarded moment. It probably dates*

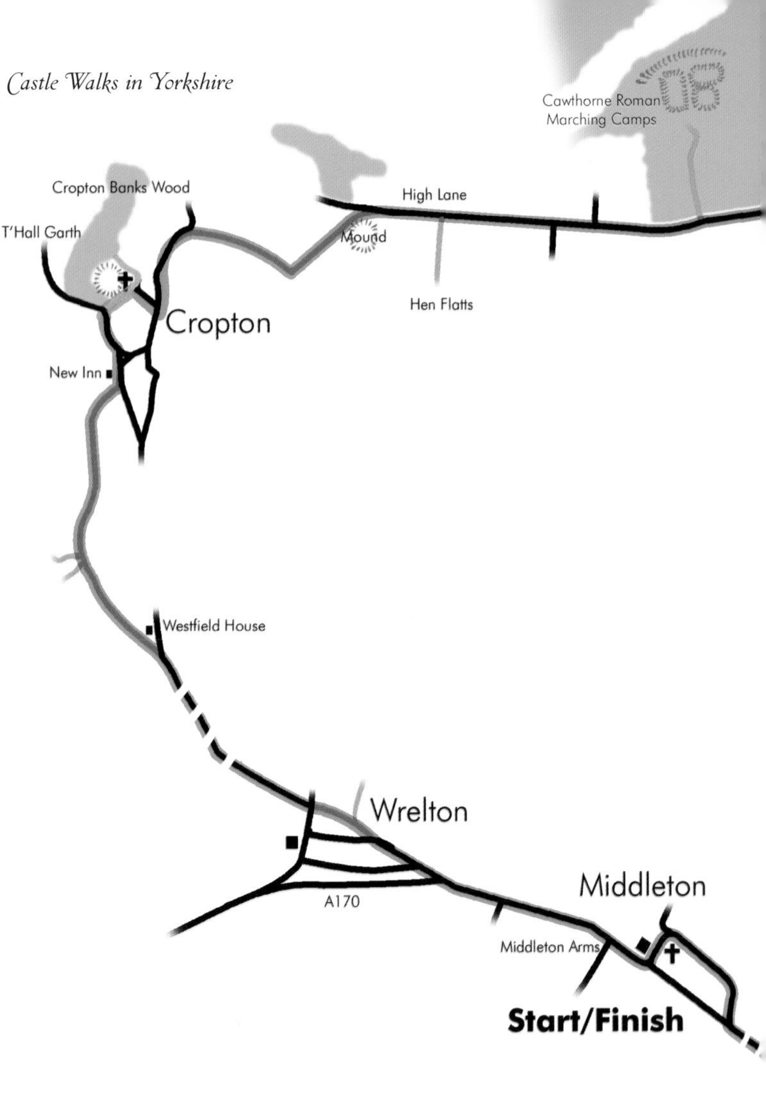

Cawthorne Roman
Marching Camps

Cropton Banks Wood

High Lane

T'Hall Garth

Mound

Cropton

Hen Flatts

New Inn

Westfield House

Wrelton

Middleton

A170

Middleton Arms

Start/Finish

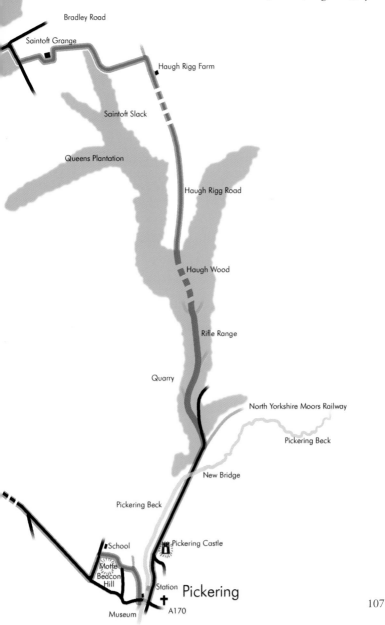

Bradley Road

Saintoft Grange

Haugh Rigg Farm

Saintoft Slack

Queens Plantation

Haugh Rigg Road

Haugh Wood

Rifle Range

Quarry

North Yorkshire Moors Railway

Pickering Beck

New Bridge

Pickering Beck

School

Pickering Castle

Motte
Beacon
Hill

Station

Pickering

Museum

A170

Bailey Hill, Pickering.

from the reign of King Stephen (1135–56) during which time England experienced a bloody civil war. The motte stands on a small knoll with remains of its ditch, while below to the east are traces of the bailey.

Follow the footpath round the playing fields to the right, to the top of a street. Turn left, and follow the path down the hill to a stile, and then veer down the bank to the right. Join a track on the left but keep ahead to the road.

Beck Isle Museum of Rural Life celebrates the local history of this typical market town and its surrounding area. Pickering (settlement of the family of a man called Picer) is also the setting for an annual wartime weekend each October organised by the North Yorks Moors Railway Company. The whole town goes back in time and recreates the Pickering of 1943, with the specific aim of commemorating the part played by Britain's railways during the Second World War and to honour the staff killed on duty.

Turn left over the river to the road junction.

Ahead at this point is the centre of Pickering. The Church of St Peter and St Paul contains several interesting fifteenth-century paintings, heavily restored in 1880, which feature 'George and the Dragon', 'St Christopher' and 'St Thomas a Becket'.

Turn left and walk up Park Street.

On the left is the terminus of the North Yorkshire Moors Railway. Trains run from Pickering through the moors to Goathland and Grosmont, and have regularly featured in television series, like Heartbeat, *and also in blockbuster movies, including* Harry Potter.

On reaching the raised pavement on the right, turn right to follow the signed path (Castle Road) up the hill that leads to the castle.

Pickering Castle is an almost perfect example of a classic earthen motte and bailey that was later re-built in stone. The original motte was built during the reign of William I to defend the northern lands against marauding Scots and also to guard the vast royal forest that existed here between 1100 and 1400, which abounded with wild boar and deer.

At the castle, turn left and walk down the hill to the main road.

By the thirteenth century the castle had been re-built in stone, strengthened and surrounded by an elaborate system of ditches.

Steam train, Pickering station.

Pickering Castle.

From 1267, the castle belonged to the Dukes of Lancaster, but by the visit of John Leland in 1530, it was in ruins. He noted that 'the inner courts are in ruins', and 'what remains of the castle walls do not seem to be very old'. The ruins are said to be haunted.

At the main road, turn right and follow the road across the bridge over Pickering Beck and then over the level crossing.

Shortly after the bend, turn left into New Bridge Quarry and follow the yellow marker posts along the bottom right-hand side of the site to a gate.

On the gate, a sign informs that this track leads to an 'MOD approved rifle range, in use Sundays from April to October, 9.00–17.00. No unauthorised use permitted'. Do not try this section of the walk at those specified times.

Follow the track deep into Pickering Woods until reaching a wide clearing, which is used as the rifle range area.

Three raised platforms indicate where the soldiers take up their positions while an earth bank in the far distance indicates where the targets are placed. The sign explains that these woods are still owned by the Duchy of Lancaster, the current 'Duke' being Her Majesty Queen Elizabeth II.

Walk ahead to the target area and go up the steep hill just to the left of the bare earth bank. Climb straight ahead up into the trees where the path soon levels off. Follow this track through the deciduous woods until they give way to a fir plantation. This is Haugh Wood.

Haugh Wood contains beech, sycamore, oak and silver birch, and is home to the coal tit, wren and many other bird species, as well as to fox, badger and bat.

From the gate walk directly out across the large open field to where the path meets a track called Haugh Rigg Road. Continue up the 'road' past Haugh Rigg Farm and then take the first path on the left, which runs down the right-hand side of a hedge.

Haugh Rigg is derived from the Old Scandinavian for 'high' 'ridge', and the steep-sided valleys on either side as one walks up from Pickering make this a perfect name.

Walk down the track towards the wooded valley to a large gate on the right, and then follow the edge of the wood down the hill.

The toft *suffix of Saintoft Grange refers to a section of land upon which a building stands or once stood, and over which common rights might still prevail. A 'croft' is a meadow adjacent to a building, although in Scotland it means a smallholding.*

At the bottom of the slope the track sweeps up and left to Saintoft Grange Farm. Walk round the left-hand edge of all the buildings, and then follow the track to the road.

In the Middle Ages, the large monasteries of England held vast estates of land all across the country. Not only were they religious houses, they were also self-sufficient communities with agricultural and industrial concerns, often identified by the name 'grange'.

At the road, turn right and then left around the corner of the wood onto Bradley Road. After a short distance, a track on the right leads up to Cawthorne Roman marching camps.

The 36-acre Roman site at Cawthorne, containing two forts, one with an annexe, together with a temporary camp, is a Scheduled Ancient Monument. It was originally thought to have been a practice camp, built c. AD 100, but this theory is being challenged. The earthworks overlap and some appear unfinished, but this may simply be that it was eventually deemed unsuitable for permanent occupation.

Turn right and walk up the lane to the car park and information board. A series of tracks lead through the woods, opening out onto the heather-clad earthworks of the Roman forts.

The low plants and open landscape of the forts provide the perfect habitat for Britain's only poisonous snake, the adder. The adder is found throughout Great Britain living in dry, open country. It can be recognised by the dark zigzag stripe down its back, but its venom only rarely kills humans. It hibernates from October to February.

Head around to the right and follow the marker posts around the site, before returning back to the car park.

In the woods below Cawthorne Bank is a holy spring, called the

Cawthorne Roman marching camps.

The view towards Cropton on a misty day.

Roman Well, which bubbles up from a crevice to run into a stone trough. It lies about one hundred metres west of the footbridge over the stream that leads into Elleron Lake. No doubt known to the Romans, it was also used by the inhabitants of Keldy Banks Farm until recently.

Back at the road, turn right. After about a mile, take the footpath on the left at White Thorn Caravan Park. Go through the gate and head out diagonally across the field to the right, aiming for a small clump of trees across the dip. At the fence turn right and follow it to a gate into a lane.

This whole area is dotted with tumuli. Victorian archaeologists have subjected these barrows to detailed excavation and finds have included a bronze dagger, a flint spearhead and two skeletons. Numerous beakers and food vessels have also been found, but possibly the most exciting find was a chariot, close to the Roman camps.

Follow the wooded lane until the houses of Cropton are reached. Take the right fork and then turn left down the road into the village. Just before the well on the right, turn right down the lane to the church.

St Gregory's was built in 1844 and contains an imitation Norman doorway, plus the remains of the Cropton cross. At the back of the church is Cropton motte.

T'hall Garth motte, Cropton.

To visit the motte, walk along the path to the right of the churchyard. Go through the gate and walk straight out into the field. The motte is directly ahead, just above the wooded valley of Cropton Beck.

The site is called Hallgarth Hill or T'hall Garth, a garth being an enclosure or yard attached to a house. The motte is completely overgrown, having been abandoned by the de Stuteville family not long after construction. The modern chapel of ease stands on the site of Robert de Stuteville's castle chapel. Subsequent owners built manor houses within the bailey, but these too have long since disappeared.

Return to the front of the church and turn right down the hill with the woods on the right.

The Woodlands Trust manages Cropton Banks Wood, which contain larch, Scots pine, western hemlock, Lawson Cyprus, Douglas fir, American red oak, Norway maple, sycamore and beech. The woods also hide a medieval trackway that runs north from St Gregory's Church.

At the road, turn left up the hill, and then turn right at the village green, with its magnificent oak tree and old water pump and trough, and head down the road past the New Inn.

Beer has been brewed in Cropton since 1613, and the tradition is being continued today at the New Inn, which has its own micro-brewery. The small brewery currently brews eleven different beers including the award-winning ales, 'Two Pints', 'Scoresby Stout' and 'Monkman's Slaughter'.

Keep ahead down the road and, after a short distance, take the public bridleway on the right. This is Bull Ing Lane.

As ing means a 'field', it is an obvious assumption that bulls were once kept in these fields. Walking through a field of cows can often be an unnerving experience, but cows are gentle, pastoral creatures and do not normally chase people. Bulls, too, are often very placid unless guarding their harem and calves. Just give them a wide berth. It is the young bullocks that can be a

Cropton village green.

bit frisky. These 'teenagers' are just curious and will come over to say 'hello'. However, cattle do not like dogs and so it is always best not to take one. If you must, never let it off the lead.

Follow the bridleway to where it joins the road at Westfield House. Turn right and follow the road all the way down into Wrelton. Where the road turns right, down to the village, go up the stone steps on the left at the back of the houses and follow the path beside the wall.

Wrelton is now a quiet village having been bypassed by the busy A170 road. Its name is interesting, possibly implying 'the place by the hill where criminals were hanged'.

The path drops to a stile, after which it keeps straight ahead with the back gardens still on the right. Keep right and go up the track and over another stile into the lane. Turn right and follow this back lane down to the main A170 road. Turn left.

The robin is a common sight over the whole country and is particularly associated with winter and Christmas. The story goes that the robin felt Christ's agony during the Crucifixion, and so went to pull a thorn from his brow. Some of Christ's blood fell upon the bird's breast and, from that time on, the robin was blessed for this act of heroism. It is deemed bad luck to kill a robin, and hence the furore over his death in the rhyme Who killed cock robin?

Follow the main road to Middleton, where an old artillery shell stands like a sentinel at the entrance to the village, opposite the village hall and a small pond. The Middleton Arms is a short distance ahead.

The old roadside shell, Middleton.

Sigston and Harlsey Castles, Yafforth and Northallerton Mottes

22.5 km/14 miles

Explorer 302 *Northallerton and Thirsk, Catterick and Bedale*

Start from the Fox and Hounds in Bullamoor

At the crossroads in front of the pub, walk ahead down the lane signposted 'Brompton 2 miles'.

This is Banks Lane and follows the line of the old Roman road that runs north through Bullamoor (moor where bulls are kept) from Boroughbridge.

After a short distance, take the lane on the right between the two houses. Follow the lane all the way to where it veers left to Stank Farm. At this point, go straight ahead through the gate into the field.

A 'stang' is a plot of land measuring one quarter of an acre, sometimes called a 'rood'. A rood consisted of 40 square rods, a rod measuring 16½ feet. This could be the derivation of the name 'stank'.

Follow the hedge ahead, veering left around two 'dog-legs' in the fence towards a gate at the bottom of the field. Cross the stream and go through the gate, aiming towards the buildings at Stank Hall. Just before the first house turn right down the lane with the fence on the left.

Stank Hall was once the home of the Lascelles family, who went on to become the Earls of Harewood of Harewood House. The

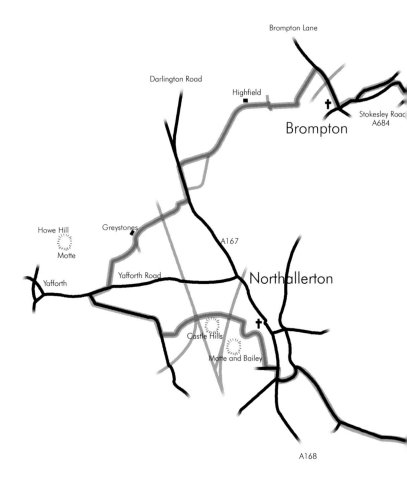

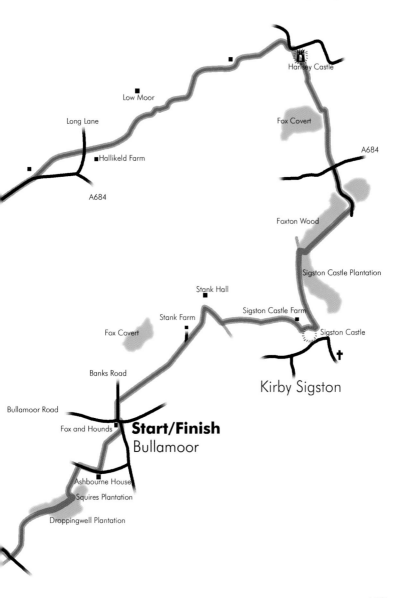

Hamsey Castle

Low Moor

Long Lane

Fox Covert

A684

Hallikeld Farm

A684

Foxton Wood

Sigston Castle Plantation

Stank Hall

Sigston Castle Farm

Stank Farm

Fox Covert

Sigston Castle

Banks Road

Kirby Sigston

Bullamoor Road

Start/Finish

Fox and Hounds

Bullamoor

Ashbourne House

Squires Plantation

Droppingwell Plantation

The view over fields towards Stank Hall.

earliest parts of the house date from 1585. The current earl's ancestors are buried in the church at Kirby Sigston. Curiously, there is also a place called Stank beside Home Farm on the Harewood Estate (see walk 4).

After passing the cricket field, turn left off the lane, and head out across a wide, open field. Continue on this line through the next two fields aiming towards the farm. Follow the path to the gate in the fence ahead, and then take the gate to the right of the farm. Walk down the lane past the buildings to a signed double gate on the left.

The village of Kirby Sigston (settlement of a man called Siggur, where there is a church) lies down the lane ahead. St Lawrence's Church contains some Norman masonry, the Lascelles' ancestors, plus a carved Viking dragon dating from the tenth century when the Danes occupied the eastern half of England.

Walk straight ahead and follow the track down the hill and round to the right.

The site of Sigston Castle is now just a series of earthworks. However, in the fourteenth century it comprised a tower and enclosure, having been granted a licence to crenellate in 1336.

The site is a Scheduled Ancient Monument and the earthworks are on private land.

At the bottom of the dip, the track veers round the marshy area to the left and back up the hill, keeping in the same field and with the hedge on the immediate right.

There are fine views here, back down to the castle site, where the ditch and ramparts are clearly visible. Beyond is the eighteenth-century tower of St Lawrence's within the village of Kirby Sigston, birthplace of actress, Dorothy Tutin.

Follow the hedge up the hill beneath the pylons to a gate. Go through, keeping the fence on the right, and head along the ridge towards the left-hand side of the wood, Sigston Castle Plantation. Follow the path up the left-hand side of the wood as it meanders right and then sharp left. At this point, a marker post indicates where to head into the trees.

St Lawrence's Church, Kirby Sigston.

Sigston Castle under snow.

The stinging nettle is very common in the Yorkshire countryside, growing on rich soils, and often around old ruins. The nettle can be quite irritating, but it is a versatile plant. Nettle stems are an ancient source of fibre for fabric and cloth and some people still cook the shoots as a spring green vegetable. It is possible to buy nettle ale, nettle wine and nettle cheese today. Nettle stings can be relieved by rubbing with the leaves of the broad-leaved dock.

Go straight down the steep bank, through the undergrowth and across the small stream. Turn left and follow the stream along the bottom of Foxton Wood all the way to the road.

Roe deer frequent these woods, but are timid animals. Quiet walkers in small groups are most likely to see them, just before they are startled and dash into the undergrowth, flashing their distinctive white rumps behind them.

At the road, turn left up the hill and follow the lane all the way to the main A684 Stokesley Road. Cross over and take the footpath directly opposite the cottage down the right-hand side of a narrow field to a gateway. Turn sharp left and then right, over the stile, by the corner of Fox Covert Wood.

Fox Covert is a common name for woods, indicating a thicket or woodland that provides shelter for game, in this case fox, but also including roe deer and pheasant.

Follow the path beside the fence to the farmyard. Go over the earthworks and out past the farm and castle to the road.

Harlsey Castle stands on a high escarpment with panoramic views over the low-lying plain to the west. In 1530, Leland noted that, at Harlsey, 'Judge Strangeways built a pretty castle'. In the fifteenth century, Sir James Strangeways of Harlsey Castle was Speaker of the House of Commons. Sir James also had land in Manchester and it was on his land that the notorious prison was built. The ditch and ramparts on the site are very much in evidence, as are the remains of the actual stone castle itself, although it may have actually been a fortified manor house. The stone undercroft is still in use today as an outbuilding, and makes a fine home for the farm's chickens.

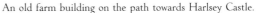

An old farm building on the path towards Harlsey Castle.

Harlsey Castle.

Turn left down the hill and, at the first bend, go straight ahead over a stile into the field. Turn right briefly and then follow an old field boundary, marked by a few straggling hawthorn trees, down the hill to the left. Keep going down the hill with the hedge and fence on the right, climbing a stile on the way to the farm.

Birds thrive in the hedgerows around these arable fields, including the linnet. The linnet is the commonest small brown finch in Britain and can be found in a wide variety of man-made habitats, often breeding in small colonies.

Walk all the way round the farm buildings to the left. Turn right and then right again through a gateway towards the house, but then turn sharp left on the other side of the hedge. Walk down the field away from the farm with the hedge on the immediate left. Keep on this line to the wooded stream. Turn left.

Looking back up to Harlsey Castle from this point, one can see pronounced evidence of medieval ridge and furrow ploughing in the field just below the castle. Compare these wide undulating ridges with the much smoother surface of a flat modern field.

Follow the stream ahead to where a marker post indicates a bridge on the right. Cross the stream and strike out over the field aiming for Low Moor Farm. After crossing the next stream, follow the field around to the left then right, coming out onto a farm lane. Cross the lane and go through the gate, walking ahead with the fence on the left to a stile in the far corner.

Across the stream on the left is Hallikeld Farm. The name means 'holy well' and may imply the location of a holy spring in this area. In Middleham, the church is dedicated to St Alkelda (see walk 14) and it is thought that her name has the same derivation.

Walk diagonally down to a stile in the bottom left-hand corner of the field, and then keep ahead through three more fields to the road, always keeping the stream on the left.

This is Long Lane, a continuation of the same Roman road from where this walk started, the course of which can be tracked quite easily on the OS maps of the area.

Turn right up the lane for a very short distance and then left into the field, aiming for a stile in the far left-hand corner. Go over the bridge on the left and then walk diagonally to the far opposite corner of the field. At the road, turn right for a short distance, before taking the next road on the right, Little Lane. The road soon turns left into the heart of the old village of Brompton.

The medieval origins of Brompton (farmstead where broom grows) can best be seen by studying the OS map. Each house that fronts the green on the left stands at the end of a long thin strip of land, deriving from the Middle Ages when agricultural land was divided into thin workable strips, rather than the large enclosed fields that we see today in most places.

Cross the footbridge on the right beside the ford, and then turn left and walk down the street to the end to where the road crosses the stream again. Turn right and walk to the crossroads with the church ahead. Turn right.

Brompton church has an interior that suggests it is of twelfth-century origin, but an over-enthusiastic restoration in 1868 has disguised or removed many ancient features. However,

St Thomas's does have a wonderful collection of hog-back tombstones and an Anglo-Danish cross from the ninth century.

Walk up Brompton Lane over the railway to a stile at the end of the hedge line on the left-hand side of the road.

Less than two miles up Brompton Lane is Standard Hill, the site of the 'Battle of the Standard'. In 1138, during the turbulent reign of King Stephen, King David of Scotland (in support of Mathilda, daughter of Henry I, who claimed the English throne) invaded and headed south. Thurstan, the archbishop of York, rallied the English troops beneath the Royal Standard and led them to a resounding victory. The vanquished dead were buried in the nearby, aptly-named, Scotspit Lane.

Walk out across the field, in a line almost parallel to the railway, aiming for a stile below where the telegraph wires cross the distant fence line. Climb the stile and cross the end of this narrow field. Turn left and follow the fence to a stile on the right.

Stephen is a little known King of England, ruling through turbulent times from 1135–54. When Henry I died (from eating too many lampreys) his daughter, Mathilda, was deemed unfit to rule; after all, she was a woman. So his nephew, Stephen of

Brompton village green.

Blois, was invited to take the throne. Naturally enough, Mathilda and her supporters were somewhat peeved, and so anarchy reigned. Only when Stephen eventually agreed to allow Mathilda's son, the future, Henry II, to accede to the throne on his death was an uneasy peace restored.

Walk round the corner of the field to the left and then follow the hedge to the track. Turn right and follow the track past the front of Highfield Farm to a gate in the hedge.

Fields called 'Poor's Land' were where the poor of the parish were entitled to gather broom or gorse (furze) for fuel, thatch, bedding and animal feed. Whereas gorse has spines, broom is spineless, and has the same uses, as well as being bundled up to make brooms, hence its name. The latter has given its name to several towns, like Brompton.

Go up the field with the hedge on the right to a stile. Veer to the left and then follow the hedge ahead towards a wood, crossing the hedge by a stile on the way to a gate.

This walk is about 14 miles long. Originally, a mile could measure anything between 4,854ft and 6,600ft. In both Scotland and Ireland it was different again. The standard mile of 5,280ft was laid down in 1593, during the reign of Elizabeth I.

Go through the gate and cross the track to a stile in the fence. Head up the slope between the plantation trees to another track, aiming for the gable ends of three large wooden buildings. Follow the track as it swings right and then left to come out in the car park of a garden centre. Walk straight ahead to the A167, Darlington Road. Turn left and just before the Northallerton sign take the footpath across the main road on the right.

Northallerton (farmstead of a man called Elfhere; the prefix 'north' was added in the thirteenth century) is a bustling market town that sits astride the main east coast railway line.

Walk across the field through a gateway, and then turn left to climb the stile in the hedge. Turn right, and walk ahead and over the railway line.

Cross the tracks with great care and pay attention to the warnings and instructions. This is the main east coast line and trains frequently pass here in excess of 100mph.

Cross the next field aiming for Greystones Farm. Take the stile and walk up the hill past the house. Go through the gate on the right and turn left down the drive. Turn left and then take the path on the right. Walk down the field keeping the hedge on the right to a stile and gate.

Over the field to the right stands Howe Hill, a 15ft-high man-made motte that sits atop an elevated platform or hillock partially surrounded by a ditch and bank. It stands near a ford over the river Whiske near the village of Yafforth (ford over the river). It is thought that the castle was destroyed or abandoned during the reign of Henry II, as documents from the reign of Richard I mention the castle in the past tense. It was probably built to guard the river crossing and to exact tolls.

Climb the stile and walk ahead with the hedge on the left to another stile. Follow the path round the building to come out on Yafforth Road. Turn right and then left down the road signposted to Romanby.

Romanby is a short distance away at this point. The name is derived from a farmstead of a man called Rothmundr, and has nothing to do with the Romans. Rothmundr is a Scandinavian name and the suffix -by means 'farmstead' or 'village', indicating that this settlement dates from the ninth and tenth centuries when Danish invaders came to settle and farm the land.

Follow the road round to the left past Castle Hill Farm, and then round to the right. Just after the gas pumping station take the lane on the left to where it bears to the right. At this point take the stile on the left and walk up the hill with the fence on the left. Follow the path over two more stiles and then over the railway.

On the right is Castle Hills, the site of Northallerton's original motte and bailey castle, which was built in 1142, but destroyed in 1176. It is thought that the stone was taken to help build the Bishop's Palace beside the church in the town. When John

Yafforth motte.

Leland visited the area in 1530, he recorded that, 'no portion of the masonry is now visible'.

Go straight on to cross the next railway by the narrow concrete bridge and then turn right. Almost immediately turn left over the stream. Walk ahead down the path with a high brick wall on the left and the cemetery on the right until reaching the Oddfellows Arms public house.

The Oddfellows Arms takes its name from a trade guild whose members used to meet here many years ago. Like many trade guilds in the Middle Ages, the Order of the Oddfellows was made up of apprentices, working 'fellows' or journeymen, and masters. The guilds were made up of workers from a particular trade, but where members were few, different trades would band together as a guild of 'odd fellows'. Many such groups met in pubs, hence the name.

Walk past the gates to the cemetery, down the lane to a large car park.

A plaque on the gates of the cemetery informs that the older part of it is sited within the moat of a twelfth-century bishop's palace demolished in 1663. The palace stood within the bailey

129

Northallerton motte.

of the later motte in Northallerton, which lies in fields at the far end of the cemetery. Over to the left is All Saints' Church, an ancient building with a door dating from 1200 and an arcade of pre-1150. The church contains many Anglo-Saxon and Anglo-Danish cross fragments.

Turn right and walk round the edge of the car park to the corner where a path leads across the open green area towards the school.

Across the grass to the left is a long line of copper beech trees planted to commemorate the coronation of George VI on 12 May 1937. On the main road opposite the church stands Porch House built in 1584. This is Northallerton's oldest house. Charles I stayed here as a guest in 1640, and as a prisoner in 1647, two years before his execution.

Follow the path behind the houses, keeping the small wooded stream on the right. After a short distance the path reaches Bailey Court, which leads to the road.

At this point, it is possible to see Northallerton motte over to the right, which stands in front of the cemetery. Built in the twelfth century, it was the successor of Castle Hills, and was refortified in 1314. The cemetery now occupies the bailey.

Turn left and walk down Romanby Road to the main road. Turn right at the Durham Ox and then cross the road using the pedestrian crossing and continue to the roundabout. Follow the road round to the left, and then turn right down the Link, just before the prison. At the mini-roundabout, turn right and walk all the way down Crosby Road to its junction with Mill Hill Lane. Turn left and walk up Sandy Bank and out of the town.

The magpie, a member of the crow family, can be seen all across the county. The name is derived from two French words: margot from Marguerite, a term used for 'a gossiping woman' owing to the bird's raucous chattering; and pie from the Latin pica, *which means magpie. Pie is the modern French name of the magpie.*

Continue down the lane to its lowest point, where it crosses the stream. Turn left and take the footpath with the stream on the right. This is Dibdale. Follow the wooded stream for a short distance and then take the path into the trees on the right and cross the stream. Walk up the bank, keeping left. After a short distance, climb the stile into the field on the right. Follow the path round the field and up the hill keeping the wooded stream on the left.

Wild garlic, or ramsons, is a member of the lily family, and often carpets damp woodlands and shady banks beside woodlands. The leaves are edible and, at certain times of the year, woodlands can smell very strongly of garlic, a defence against insects and other predators.

The path veers to the left over the brow of the hill and leads to a gate. Go into the wood and follow the winding path through Dropping Well Plantation, still with the stream down to the left.

This mixed wood is filled with oak and beech trees, hawthorn bushes, and dense bramble in the undergrowth.

After a short distance, a marker post indicates where the path drops down to the left to cross the muddy stream. Keep inside the end of the wood to a gate. Go through the kissing gate into the open field on the right and follow the boundary fence round to the left and then ahead to the road, Scholla Lane.

Over to the right, the field between Ashbourne House and Squire's Plantation shows obvious signs of medieval ridge and furrow ploughing, similar to that at Harlsey Castle. When the sun is low the long shadows make such features on the landscape far easier to see.

Go over the stile to the left of the gate and turn right. Opposite Ashbourne House, turn left up the gravel drive, passing through two gates. Walk along the bottom of what has become someone's garden, and through the high wooden fence in the far left-hand corner.

The importance of fox hunting to some in the countryside is apparent in the many inns that bear the name 'Fox and Hounds'. Turning the cull of so-called pests into a sport is rather barbaric and archaic. In medieval times, the sign of the 'Dog and Bear' indicated that bear-baiting was offered as entertainment. Thankfully, bear-baiting, like cock-fighting, is no longer available at wayside hostelries.

Keeping the fence on the left, walk ahead to a gateway. Go through and then turn half right and walk to the large field gate that leads onto the road. Turn left and the Fox and Hounds is a short distance ahead.

Castleton and Kildale Mottes, and Danby Castle

27.5 km/17 miles

Explorer OL26 *North York Moors, Western area*

Start from the Fox and Hounds in Ainthorpe

Ainthorpe is derived from the Scandinavian for an 'outlying farmstead', thorpe of a man called 'Einulf ', indicating that these moorland areas were colonised by Danish settlers in the ninth and tenth centuries.

Walk down the hill, using an ancient worn pavement on the left-hand side of the road, to the small triangular green. Turn left down the narrow road in front of Lilac Terrace and follow this road all the way to the main road. Turn left.

The age of this footpath can be guessed from the wearing that has taken place over the centuries. The fact that this path is paved with such large blocks of stone implies that this was an important trade route across the landscape for merchants and packhorses.

Follow the road towards Castleton and, as the road drops sharply down to the right, go straight ahead along the footpath below 'The Howe'. At the war memorial, take the right-hand fork in front of the monument.

Walk along the flat green terrace and then drop left down the steep bank to a stream. Cross the footbridge and follow the path up the other side, coming out opposite the church.

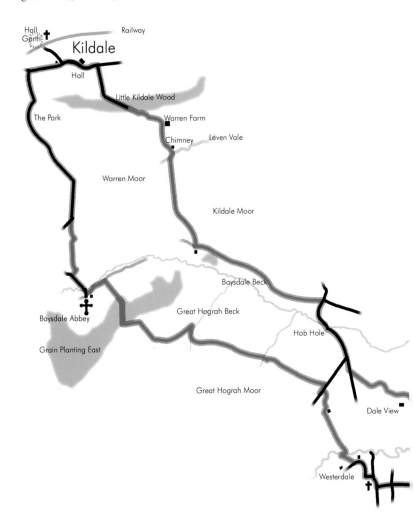

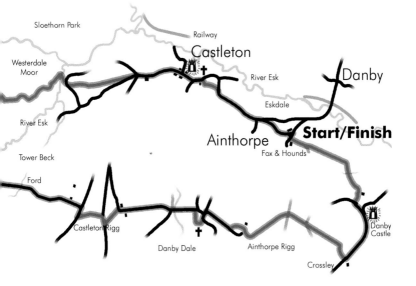

This is the Church of St Michael and St George in the village of Castleton (settlement with a castle).

Turn left and walk up the hill into the centre of the town, passing the junction with Castle Hill on the right.

About 100 metres down this road is Castle Hill, an impressive modern house with a tower built on the site of the castle. Castleton motte is a small, strong projection on the hillside high above the River Esk. The site comprises a massive bank on the exposed side and a counter-scarp bank, which seems to have been a partial ringwork, although much damaged. It is thought to have had strong masonry defences including walls 13 feet thick, and was the predecessor to Danby Castle. It was mentioned in 1242, but recorded as a ruined peel tower by 1336.

Walk all the way up High Street through the village, passing the Moorlands Country House Hotel on the way.

Opposite the hotel is a sign that says, 'No tipping, by order Danby Court Leet'. Traditionally, a court leet was a medieval court held in a lordship every six months in the presence of the lord of the manor. It had jurisdiction over petty offences and civil affairs of the district and could fine and imprison offenders. It also performed a wide variety of administrative duties such as appointing a local constable.

At the top of the hill head down the narrow road signposted 'Westerdale 1¾ miles, gated road'. Almost

Ancient paved track, Ainthorpe.

immediately, take the footpath on the right and strike out along the moor, keeping a line of white-topped posts just to the right. The path eventually begins to drop and meets a wall on the left.

There are three main heathers in the heath family. Ling is probably the most common variety and is found almost everywhere, characterised by dense, tiny leaves and solitary flowers. Bell heather is common on dry heaths and moors and has bell-shaped flowers. Cross-leaved heath is most common on wet heaths and moors and is distinguished by its four small, narrow pointed leaves arranged in whorls of four.

Follow the wall for a short distance before heading right, down a wide green path. Cross over the road to the left and take the continuation of the green track down to a path on the left, just before the gate, that leads to the stream. Cross the bridge and head up the bank to the left, passing through a small stand of wind-swept oak and silver birch to meet the corner of the wood at the top of the hill.

The moor is covered with isolated, solitary boulders, set amid a sea of bilberry, heather, and grouse shooting butts.

Modern battlemented house on Castleton motte.

Follow the wall up around the wood, keeping the wall on the immediate left at all times. Follow this wall all along the moor as it rises and falls around small plantations of silver birch and Scots pine. The path is signed. At the gate, turn right and walk up the hill by the wall, following it round to the left. The path soon rises up towards the open moor once more, and a signpost indicates that this is part of the Esk Valley Walk.

The Esk Valley Walk follows the River Esk from its source high on the North York Moors to the coast at Whitby, and takes walkers through varied countryside, from open moorland to farmland pastures. The walk is clearly waymarked for most of the way with 'leaping salmon' signs.

At the back of the farm the wall begins to drop away to the left, but the path continues straight ahead until it eventually rejoins the wall. After about 50 metres the path turns right, up to the moor, where a cairn marks its junction with a wider track. Turn left and follow the cairned track to a footpath sign on the road.

These moors are a breeding ground for the red grouse, as indicated by the shooting butts. The red grouse has a vivid red flash on its head above the eye, and can startle walkers with its loud cackling cry as it flies low over the heather.

Turn right and follow the road all the way down to the ford at Hob Hole. Cross the river by the footbridge and walk up the other side to the junction. Turn left along the bridleway.

The North Yorkshire Moors National Park is one of the most beautiful areas of England, and contains the largest expanse of heather moorland in the country. It is a treasured landscape and fully deserves all the care the nation can give it. Despite being a National Park most of the land is privately owned, although visitors are free to explore using the extensive network of footpaths and bridleways.

Follow the bridleway all along the hillside for about 1½ miles to a solitary barn.

Kildale Moor is covered with evidence of Stone Age settlements, field systems and enclosures, including sixty small cairns.

At the barn, turn right up to a cairn on the top of the hill. Follow the path over the moor, aiming directly for Captain Cook's monument in the far distance to the north-west, passing a marker post on the way to a wall. Go through the gate and veer right to walk down the slope, heading for a solitary industrial chimney in the valley below. Walk down the two fields to the sparse wood in the valley. Cross the stream and follow the farm track up the hill past the chimney to Warren Farm.

The chimney is all that remains of Warren Moor ironstone mine, although the map shows the line of a disused railway that once served this remote industrial site.

Go through the gate to the left of the farmhouse and follow the lane past the trees, as it turns left through the wood and then right, down to the road. Turn left into Kildale.

Kildale is an estate village and has only had three owners in the last 800 years. Virtually all the farms and houses are still owned by the estate, where ironstone and whinstone was mined.

The slight mound of Kildale motte.

At the triangular green in the centre of the village keep straight ahead up the road, passing the junction on the right that leads to the church and site of Kildale Castle.

In the twelfth century, the Percy family built a castle here that was later replaced by a manor house, only a few stones of which now remain in the current house, Hall Garth, built upon the low motte. West of the church is the oval motte, partly cut by the railway. St Cuthbert's Church is reached by footbridge across the Middlesbrough to Whitby railway. The porch contains tombstones to the Percy family, former Lords of the Manor, whose name lives on in Percy Rigg and Percy Cross. The current church, rebuilt in 1868, stands on the site of former churches dating back to Saxon and Norman times. Viking burials were discovered beneath the floor of the previous church.

Walk up the hill out of the village and take the first road on the left, signed Baysdale Farm and Cleveland Way. Follow this single-track road all the way up the hill around a craggy outcrop on the left called The Park.

Looking back from this point, Captain Cook's monument is visible on the wooded hillside opposite. Standing 51ft high, the obelisk is made of local sandstone and was erected in 1827 by Robert Campion of Whitby to commemorate the life of Captain James Cook, who was born in nearby Great Ayton. The inscription reads: 'A man in nautical knowledge inferior to none, in zeal, prudence and energy superior to most, regardless of danger he opened an intercourse with the friendly isles and other parts of the southern hemisphere'. Cook is remembered as the man who discovered Australia, but the Aborigines probably already knew it was there.

Turn right along the road to the gate and, where the road bends to the right, keep ahead. The route leaves the Cleveland Way at this point.

The Cleveland Way is a 109-mile/176km-long national trail that starts in Helmsley and follows the edge of the North Yorkshire

Moors north to the coast at Saltburn-by-the-Sea, before following the cliffs and bays south to Filey.

Take the path over the moor and follow a series of old fence posts down the hill. At the wall go around the corner on the right and continue down the hill to a gate. Go through the gate and veer right and then left to follow the stream down to another gate. Go through the gate and keep to the left-hand side of the field, down to the track. Turn right to the road, and then left down the hill to Baysdale Abbey.

Baysdale Abbey Farm is built on the original site of a thirteenth-century Cistercian nunnery that existed from 1190 to 1539. All that remains today is the small stone bridge over Black Beck. Datestones in the current building are from 1653 and 1812. The name is derived from 'bas' and 'dale', and was recorded in Yorkshire charters of 1189 and 1204, meaning 'cow-shed valley'.

Go over the old bridge and then turn left after the first barn. Go between the farm buildings to the left to a farm track, and then follow the track round to the left as it follows the wooded stream down Baysdale. At the gate turn right up the hill towards Thorntree House. Go through the gateway on the left just after the barn, and then turn right up the hill beside the wood.

In the Middle Ages, land rents in Baysdale were paid with the wolves' heads, indicating how numerous these animals were at the time.

Half way up the hill, turn right into the wood and follow the wide forestry road to the open moor. Go over a stile and turn left. Follow the top of the wood until a wall is reached. Go through the gateway and then turn right, up the hill, gradually moving away from the wall. Aim for a cairn over the brow of the hill, and then follow the path as it begins to veer off down to the left. The path slowly descends until it meets a track. Follow the track down to the left aiming for a small wooded ravine down which Great Hograh Beck flows.

The North Yorkshire Moors National Park covers 554 sq miles (1,436 sq km) and contains the largest expanse of open heather moorland in England and Wales.

The heather-clad moors above Baysdale Abbey.

At the top of the wood, walk back down a path on the right to the footbridge, across which is a stone memorial to a fellow walker. Go straight ahead up onto the moor, following the path to another memorial cairn on the nearby skyline. The cairned path, called Skinner Howe Cross Road, now roughly follows the contours of Great Hograh Moor, high above Baysdale down to the left, crossing a couple of streams on its way to the road on Little Hograh Moor, about 1½ miles away.

For over 65 million years, the hills of the North Yorkshire Moors have been slowly rising, creating the landscape of hills and dales of today. The wide dales, like Baysdale, were carved out by torrents of melting glacial ice, although the rivers that flow the same course now are much smaller.

At the road turn right down to a footpath sign on the left. Keep the wall on the right for a short distance, and then turn right down the hill. At the bottom of the wall take the stile in the corner on the right. Turn left down the hill towards Brown House, taking the gate in the wall just beyond the house. Follow the sign for Westerdale and walk straight ahead down the fields to the young River Esk.

The Esk may look harmless here but it can rise to flood levels, as it did in November 2000, flooding houses and sweeping away fences, trees, even whole sections of stone walls. In 1930/31 the Esk flood was so great that it swept away many of the road and rail bridges further down the valley. The old road bridge over the Esk is medieval, but is no longer used.

Go over the footbridge and then turn right up the farm track that swings round to the top of the bank. In the field, aim for the large solitary tree over the brow of the hill, half way between the tower of the Lodge on the left and Hall Farm over to the right.

Westerdale Hall has an impressive pele tower and was built as a baronial shooting lodge for the Duncombes of Duncombe Park in Helmsley (see walk 7) sometime around 1874. The village borders some fine grouse shooting moors, and so this makes an ideal base.

At the road turn left and follow it right and then left over the wooded stream to come out in the centre of the village by the church. Turn right up the hill and then first left.

The river Esk near Westerdale Hall.

Christ Church in Westerdale ('more westerly dale') has a Norman tympanum in the west tower. However, the church was heavily restored during the Victorian period, a common practice for many parish churches that, despite good intentions, destroyed many original features. Just south of the church is a house called Arkangel, in which is the Bulmer monument of 1727, a memorial to Thomas Bulmer, a sailor.

Walk down Christy Gate Road, go straight over at the crossroads, and then follow the lane all the way down the hill over the ford and back up the other side to the road just beyond Quarry Farm.

Turn right briefly, and then left up a footpath that leads onto the top of Castleton Rigg – this path is not signed – and ahead to the road.

Scandinavian settlement in this area is most noticeable in the names of villages and geographic features. For example, the Norse for 'ridge' is rigg, *'waterall' is* foss *and* kirkja *means a 'farmstead by the church'.*

Cross the road and then walk down the green gulley that slants left down to the road beside Crag House Farm. Go through the gate and follow the road all the way to the church, crossing Danby Beck on the way. Take the footpath on the right over the field that leads directly to the Church of St Hilda.

St Hilda's Church contains sections from many different centuries, including an eighteenth-century gallery reached by external steps and the Royal Arms of King George IV, who reigned from 1820–30. As Prince Regent, he was a reckless womaniser and extravagant dandy, but his legacy was the Brighton Pavilion and the British Library. He was a great fan of Jane Austen and Sir Walter Scott.

Turn left up the gravelled drive, and then walk back up to the road. Go straight ahead past the junction on the right and keep ahead at the bend down Tofts Lane.

A 'toft' is a plot of land on which a building once stood, as opposed to a 'croft', which is an enclosed meadow adjacent to a house. Common rights might still be attached to the house

The ford on the quiet lane to Quarry Farm.

and plot of land even though the building itself may have long since disappeared.

Almost immediately turn right down the lane towards North End Farm. Take the footpath on the left just after the first barn and walk across the field to a series of stone steps that lead into the next field. Walk diagonally over to the right and go through the gate in the bottom left-hand corner. Cross the marshy section of land to a wooden footpath sign by a lane. Go straight over the lane and through the gate as indicated and walk up towards the back of the farm. The path swings behind the house and then left up the hill.

Hares frequent these heathery slopes. They can be distinguished from their smaller cousins (rabbits) by size – hares being much larger – and by their black-tipped ears. Whereas a rabbit will not stray far from its burrow and soon disappears if startled, a hare does not live below ground and will race away at great speed if surprised.

Follow the wall up towards the moor and then turn left across the top of another wall. Follow this wall along to its highest point and, where it begins to drop, head up the path aiming for a series of former quarries on the moor, indicated by irregular spoil heaps on the skyline ahead. Near the top of the hill the path is paved, probably from the days when these quarries were active.

This path is marshy in places although the wettest sections can be avoided by looking out for the soft rush, which has a long sharply pointed stem and a brown flower about a third of the way down.

At the top of the hill veer off to the right aiming for a solitary marker post standing on a footpath that runs the full length of Ainthorpe Rigg, from where there are great views in all directions.

A solitary standing stone marks a series of settlements and field systems up the moor. There are many such features in this area from a time when people settled on the hilltops for security, rather than in later centuries when valleys provide water for power, wood for fuel and shelter from the elements.

Cross this wide path at 90° and strike out across the heather moorland. The bank drops down to the left, so keep along the path that follows the contours to another marker post. At this point, aim for the top right-hand end of the wall in the far distance.

A series of paths criss-cross this moor, so if the wall is reached before the top end simply turn right and follow the stone wall to the brow of the hill. It can be confusing in mist. Danby (village of the Danes) is clearly visible down the valley to the left.

The path continues to cross the moorland, and rises gradually, with the highest part of the moor up to the right. The well-defined path leads to the far right-hand end of the wall ahead, and is marked by a cairn.

The stone walls in this region are made of quiet substantial square or cubic blocks of local stone which seem to be too uniform to be natural. When compared to the smaller more

Danby Castle.

fragmented sandstone used in West Yorkshire, the walls in this area look as if each stone has been individually shaped by man.

Drop straight down the steep bank of Crossley Side to the road beside Crossley Gate Farm, in the glacial valley of Fryup. Turn left and follow the road round below the crags to Danby Castle Farm.

Danby Castle is a small, compact quadrangular castle, with angle towers projecting diagonally. It was the late-fourteenth century successor to the motte at Castleton, which was also called Danby in early references. Danby was the home of the de Brus, Latimer and Neville families, as well Catherine Parr with her second husband, Lord John Latimer, in the sixteenth century before she became the sixth wife of Henry VIII. Today, the remains of Danby Castle are at the centre of a working farm and the farmhouse itself is an extension of the south-west wing. An Elizabethan justice's throne stands in the upper floor solar.

Follow the road round keeping the craggy escarpment on the immediate left. After a short distance turn right through the gate leading down to Castle Houses Farm.

View over Eskdale.

Danby Moors is a 'common' that is still administered by the original feudal court, the Danby Court Leet, which is based at the original administrative centre in Danby Castle. The court and jury rooms are still in regular use.

Walk down past the first barn and then veer to the left around the other buildings. Walk down to a stile and signpost opposite a gate that leads into the farmyard. At this point turn sharp left and walk across the field to a ladder stile beside a gate.

The fields are often spread with farm manure throughout the winter. This is to ensure that the April showers wash the nutrients into the soil so that crops sown in the spring will gain the full benefit.

Walk straight down the next field into the bottom corner where a small gate leads over the stream. Go straight ahead up the next field and over the brow of the hill to the hedge. Turn left and follow the hedge along to another small gate.

Just outside the village of Danby is the Moors Visitor Centre, which opened in 1976. It is housed in the former shooting lodge of the Dawnay family, whose ancestors still own the estate. The house could not accommodate large parties, but acted merely as a base for small parties who participated in field sports with Lord Downe. Duck Bridge in the valley is a medieval packhorse bridge over the River Esk. The Neville family coat of arms can still be seen on the parapet.

Once through the gate, turn left over a stile. Follow the edge of the field round to the left and then right. Walk straight ahead until confronted by a stile. Go over the stile and keep ahead to the end of the wall.

Cow parsley is a member of the carrot family, and is a common sight down rural lanes and farm tracks across the countryside. It is a robust perennial with tall, branched stems and small white flowers massed in flat-topped heads or umbrels. Although edible, it is related to the poisonous hemlock. It is also know as Queen Anne's lace.

In the corner of the field take the stile on the left. Walk up the path to another stile and then turn right up the lane. This lane leads all the way back into Ainthorpe. At the road turn left, and the Fox and Hounds is a short distance up the hill.

Scarborough and Ayton Castles and Manor Garth, Seamer

24 km/15 miles

Explorer OL27 *North York Moors, Eastern area,*
Explorer 301 *Scarborough and Bridlington*

Start from Ye Old Forge Valley Inn in West Ayton

*The word 'ye' is almost always misinterpreted as an
archaic form of 'you'. In fact, in this context, 'ye' simply
means 'the'. In Old English, the language of the Anglo-
Saxons, there was a specific symbol that looked something
like a 'y' that was used to signify 'th' and pronounced 'th'.
When later scribes wrote this down they mistook it for
a 'y' and hence this common error.*

From the pub turn right (east) and head across the A170 road bridge over the River Derwent.

> *The bridge of four arches was built in 1775 by John Carr. The
> name of the village, Ay-ton, is derived from the Old English
> language of the Anglo-Saxons, farmstead* tun *on a river* ea, *in
> this case the Derwent.*

Follow the main road through the village into East Ayton to the roundabout beside the church.

> *This is the Church of St John the Baptist, which contains
> Norman and Anglo-Saxon remnants.*

Turn right at this point down the narrow lane to where it turns sharply to the left. This is Long Lane. Follow it all the way along beside the river Derwent, where it becomes Carr Fields Lane. Keep straight ahead.

> *Over the fields to the left is Irton, the 'farmstead of the Irishmen'. This settlement would have been given its name by incoming Scandinavian settlers who would have found a village of Britons, or Irish, (i.e. Celtic people) already living here.*

Almost at the end of the lane, turn left over a stile and walk in a straight line toward Seamer, skirting round to the left of Outgang Plantation. The path reaches the end of a lane. Turn left and then right to the main road.

> *A 'carr' is a northern term for a marshy meadow. One possible meaning for 'outgang' is a field that was not always kept in cultivation, another is that it alludes to a path running close by, as there is in this case. Down beside the river Derwent, the field names – ings, holms, carr and flats – all indicate that this area is historically prone to flooding.*

Turn left towards the church and then take a slight detour through the open access field on the left to visit the remains of Manor Garth behind the church.

Old barn, Long Lane, Ayton.

The remains of Manor Garth, Seamer.

This is all that is left of a medieval manor house, dating from the early fourteenth century. Ruined walls and earth-works indicate that it was possibly a dower house or tower house. A 'dower' house is the home given to the wi-dow of a lord after their son had taken over and moved into the lord's seat. In 1547 it was recorded as a castle.

Return to the road and continue on through the village past the church. At the roundabout turn right and then left up Stoney Haggs Road and over the hill to where it meets the A64 (T).

Selfheal is a common plant but thrives on good soil in hedgerows and waysides. It has rich pinky-purple flowers set in dark bracts and can sprawl or grow erect to 20ins. The name reflects its use as a medicinal herb to staunch and heal wounds.

Cross directly over the main road and turn right to a large roundabout. Turn left following the sign for Eastfield, and then, almost immediately, turn left up the farm track leading to High Eastfield Farm, signed 'Bridleway to High Deepdale'. Where the track turns right towards the farm, keep straight ahead up the rough track, passing gorse bushes on the left to a marker post before a wide, open field.

From March until October, the bright yellow flowers of the gorse are a common sight on moors and heaths and in hedgerows and embankments of poor soil. It regenerates well after burning and was a major source of fuel in the rural economy for many centuries.

Walk directly over the field to the right-hand edge of Oliver's Mount Farm. Turn right and then left along the track to meet the road, with Deepdale down to the right. Go straight down the road and keep ahead over the crossroads with the golf club on the right.

The story goes that the name golf comes from the acronym 'Gentlemen Only, Ladies Forbidden', but there may be those who would like to dispute this! The truth is that the origins of the name golf are unknown.

Cross directly over the main A165 road, down Seacliffe Road, and then carry straight on to the clifftop car park.

The barren space on the left is the site of the former Holbeck Hall Hotel, which fell into the sea in 1993. The cliffs along this section of the east coast are prone to landslips. The first landslide was in December 1737 and was reported as an earthquake. An acre of land on which five cows were grazing suddenly slipped down the cliffs. The cows were unhurt. Over one hundred and fifty years later in 1892–93 there were three further landslides.

Turn right into the car park and then take the path over the grassy bank on the left towards the sea. Walk down the hill to a junction, and take the left fork towards the beach with Scarborough beyond.

Holbeck Hall was built as a private house in 1880 for fishing magnate George Alverson Smith, despite being advised against this site. It took three days for the hotel and grounds to fall into the sea in 1993. Since then, there have been extensive consolidation and stabilisation projects to ensure the cliffs remain secure.

Follow the path to the concrete walkway, which joins the seafront promenade. If the tide is out it is possible to walk all the way round to the harbour on the beach. If not, follow the promenade.

The cliffs at the southern end of South Shore are mid-Jurassic rocks capped with boulder clay. Sedimentary rocks are visible

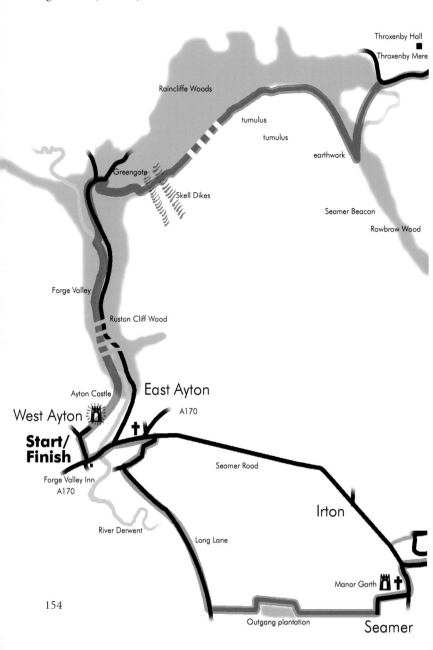

Throxenby Hall

Throxenby Mere

Raincliffe Woods

tumulus

tumulus

earthwork

Greengate

Skell Dikes

Seamer Beacon

Rowbrow Wood

Forge Valley

Ruston Cliff Wood

Ayton Castle

East Ayton

A170

West Ayton

**Start/
Finish**

Forge Valley Inn
A170

Seamer Road

Irton

River Derwent

Long Lane

Manor Garth

Outgang plantation

Seamer

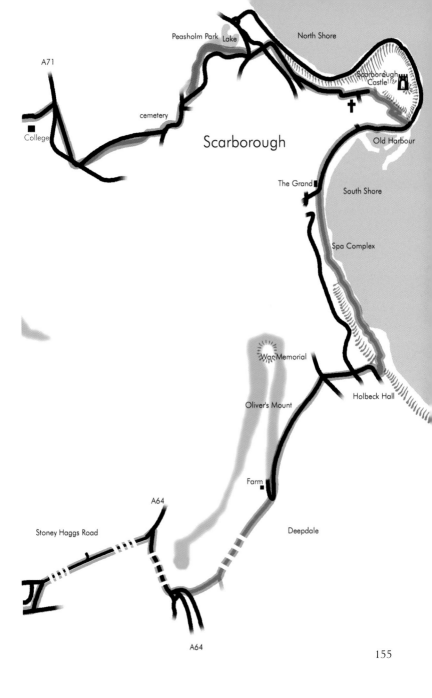

Scarborough

A71

College

cemetery

Peasholm Park Lake

North Shore

Scarborough Castle

Old Harbour

The Grand

South Shore

Spa Complex

War Memorial

Oliver's Mount

Holbeck Hall

Farm

A64

Stoney Haggs Road

Deepdale

A64

155

South Bay, Scarborough from Holbeck.

in the lower parts of the cliffs, comprised of grey Scarborough formation below, and sandstone above. Scarborough formation is comprised of sandstone, limestone and shale. The boulder clay that caps it regularly slips down and obscures the older strata. Look out for seabirds, flying above the cliffs and waves. It is often possible to see several variety of seagull, plus cormorant, shag, razorbill, guillemot and puffin, making their way out to sea to fish, or back to the cliffs where they breed.

If the waves are too rough, there is a cliffside path through the gardens above. Whichever route is preferred, the aim is to reach the slipway at the far side of the south shore beach below the castle.

The streams that enter the sea in Scarborough are spanned by two impressive bridges. Valley Bridge was built in 1865 and widened in 1926 for road traffic. The Spa Bridge of 1826–27 is a cast iron footbridge, high above the valley, and 414 feet long.

Continue past the harbour on the main seafront road until the Coast Guard station is reached.

There are three piers in the harbour. The Old Pier is in the middle to which St Vincent's Pier was added in 1732 with a lighthouse of 1800 (rebuilt after 1914). The East Pier was added in c.1790–1812 and the West Pier in 1897.

At this point go up the steps on the left signed 'Castle'.

The walk passes the centre of Scarborough (stronghold of a man called Skarthi) with its spa complex and the funicular railways on either side of the Grand Hotel. This grand Victorian hotel was built by Cuthbert Brodrick in 1867, to a 'calendar' design, having a dome for each season, a floor for each month, a chimney for each week and a room for every day of the year. Amid the tacky seafront amusement arcades, gift shops and seafood sellers, stands the historic Richard III Inn, where the then future king is reputed to have stayed some 500 years ago. However, it is Elizabethan, not medieval.

After a short distance a path veers up to the right, signposted 'Castle Walls'. Follow this path to the walls overlooking the harbour, and then turn back to walk all the way up below the castle walls to the main castle entrance.

The impressive ruins of Scarborough Castle dominate the town. The twelfth-century tower and curtain walls stand behind the impregnable gatehouse and bridge into the castle, built on a natural promontory. Within the bailey there was also a Roman signal station, Our Lady's Well and the site of the town's very first church to St Mary. Leland was impressed by the 'exceedingly good large and strong castle on a steep rock' and the entrance with its 'two towers and betwixt each of them a drawbridge, having steep rock on each side of them'. The 100ft-high keep was built on the orders of Henry II between 1138–64. During the Civil War the castle was besieged, taken and reduced. Just as Henry VIII was responsible for the needless destruction of so many of the great monasteries of England, so Cromwell should be vilified for the destruction of so many wonderful castles.

Walk down the road leading directly away from the castle entrance, passing two castellated mansions on the right.

The tower, Scarborough Castle.

These grand houses, 'The Towers' and 'The Castle by the Sea', were both built in the 1960s.

Continue ahead with the graveyard on the left, which contains the grave of Anne Brontë.

Anne Brontë, along with her sisters Charlotte and Emily, was a fine writer, and her two most famous novels were The Tenant of Wildfell Hall *and* Agnes Grey. *She came to Scarborough from Haworth already dying of tuberculosis and, after only a few days here, she died on 28 May 1849. Unlike the rest of the family she is not buried in the family tomb at Haworth but in St Mary's churchyard overlooking the sea she loved so much. Charlotte only re-visited the grave once, on 4 June 1852, a few days after the third anniversary of Anne's death. She did not stay long in Scarborough, but spent the following few weeks near Filey.*

Walk past the church and turn right after the Albion public house, and then left down a high terrace overlooking the North Sands.

St Mary's, the parish church of Scarborough, was begun c.1170–1200 and was originally built with imposing twin towers, possibly by the stonemasons who built the castle. Extensions and alterations, including the removal of the twin towers, were carried out during the fourteenth century. The central tower and the chancel were destroyed by artillery during the Civil War when the Parliamentarians used the church

St Mary's church, Scarborough.

for their batteries to attack the Royalist-held castle. The existing tower was rebuilt in 1670 and the extent of the original chancel is marked through the graveyard by masonry.

Follow this road, Queen's Parade, with its brightly coloured B&Bs, all the way down to the Crispin Hotel. Follow the road round to the left and down to the main road. Cross directly over and walk down Victoria Park.

Of particular artistic note in the town is the Church of St Martin on Albion Road. It contains much pre-Raphaelite work, including a pulpit described as 'gem'. It is adorned with ten painted panels by Rosetti, Ford Madox Brown and William Morris.

Cross straight over Columbus Ravine and enter Peasholme Park. Walk down to the lake and turn left, and keep going until reaching the stream. Follow the stream up into the wooded valley staying on the path on the left-hand side. After a while the path crosses to the right-hand bank via a stone bridge, and then back again.

It is hard to imagine that this deep wooded valley is in the centre of a busy town. Although the lake section is heavily manicured and decorated in an oriental theme, the narrow valley is wilder and far more natural looking.

The path crosses to the right-hand bank once more and, at the next junction, keep left. Another stone bridge leads back over the stream and the path starts climbing the high bank to come out on the road. Turn right and walk up to the main road. Take the second road off the mini-roundabout on the left, called Manor Road. Walk past the cemetery and then follow the road round to the right and then left, past the quaint red-brick cemetery chapel and house of 1902.

England is a small country and many churchyards and cemeteries have long been full to overflowing. In the seventeenth and eighteenth centuries many coffins were dug up and the bones piled in a 'bonehouse', freeing up space in the graveyard. However, it was noticed that 1 in 25 coffins had scratches on the inside indicating that many people had been buried alive! To make sure that this did not happen again, a bell was buried with the 'corpse'. Someone would then sit all night by the grave to see if the bell rang, and if so, the incumbent was dug up, having been 'saved by the bell'. Allegedly ...

At the next roundabout, turn right to cross the line of the old railway and walk up the hill. After a short distance cross to the left-hand side of the road and enter the small wooded park. Turn right and follow the path through the trees to the end of the wood, coming out at the top of Woodland Ravine. Cross over Woodland Ravine and turn left to the busy Scalby Road. Turn right past an overgrown archway and St Catherine's Hospice.

A plaque on the archway reads: 'These homes for gentle people of reduced circumstance are built in accordance with the will of Francis Grey Smart in remembrance of his father John Cass Smart and of himself, that they may prove a place of rest and comfort for many weary ones, 1931'.

Continue up the main road and then turn right up what is actually a continuation of Scalby Road, which leads back to the main road. Cross over and turn right, then left round the college playing fields. Walk all the way up this road, Lady Edith's Drive, signposted to 'The Forge Valley'. Just before Throxenby Mere, where the road turns sharp right, turn left up a bridleway past a group of ramshackle farm buildings. The track starts to climb the steep hillside, called Rowbrow Wood, and where the main track veers left, keep straight ahead to the top of the steep wooded escarpment.

The wood contains mature beech, Scot's pine and silver birch, and is carpeted with bluebell in the spring.

Turn right at the top and follow the edge of the woodland all the way round this flat plateau, called Seamer Moor. After a few hundred metres, the path continues around the edge of the wood but just inside a wall, eventually crossing two parallel ditches.

This whole landscape is dotted with tumuli and other earthworks, including these ditches, known as Skell Dykes, which run for some considerable distance over the landscape.

A short distance after the dykes the path reaches a gate that leads out into the fields. At this point, continue to the right, staying along the top of the wood inside the fence. At the first junction, take the path that leads down the steep slope. Keep going down to where it meets

Skell Dykes on Seamer Moor.

The raised path through the Forge Valley.

another path, turn left and continue down some wooden steps and over a wooden bridge.

This is the Forge Valley, a wildlife haven for birds, small mammals, insects and butterflies. The name 'butterfly' comes from the Old English buttorfleoge and the Dutch word boterschijte, meaning 'buttershite', derived from the unappealing fact that a butterfly's excrement looks both creamy and yellow, like butter!

At the next junction, turn right and follow this path all the way down to a small car park beside the road. Turn left down the road to a junction and turn left again. Follow the road round to the left and walk ahead with the wooded stream on the right.

Just over the stream at this point is the holy spring of Old Man's Mouth. The name comes from the mouth-like orifice from which the water pours into a stone trough, although it was called Scarwell Springs on the OS map.

After passing a small layby, the road reaches a small car park on the right. Head into the car park and turn right, to where a bridge leads over the river Derwent. Cross over and turn left down the raised wooden walkway.

> *The walkway has been built to allow wheelchair and pushchair access to the riverside nature reserve, which contains some of the best indigenous woodland in North Yorkshire.*

Follow the walkway to a gate and stile. Climb the stile and walk ahead into the field. Follow the fence round the bottom edge of the wood on the right. Eventually, the track leads up the bank on the right and into a field and past the remains of Ayton Castle.

> *Ayton Castle is a late-fourteenth century, three-storey, stone tower-house, with rib-vaulted chambers and twin mural stairs to give access to the upper floors. One corner stands to the height of the wall-head, where surviving corbels give evidence of a machicolated parapet and a corner turret. To the east are the remnants of the inner and outer bailey ramparts, with the grass-covered foundations of an inner gateway and traces of fishponds down towards the river.*

Walk past the castle and head through the gate into Castle Rise. At the road turn left down Yedmandale Road, back to the starting point.

Ayton Castle.

Mulgrave Castle and Lythe Motte

23.5 km/14.5 miles

Explorer OL27 *North York Moors, Eastern area*

Start from the Hart Inn in Sandsend

IMPORTANT NOTE: Mulgrave Woods are only open on Saturdays, Sundays and Wednesdays, and are closed throughout the month of May.

From the pub turn left and cross the road bridge over East Beck. Turn left almost immediately and walk through the car park to the gate. Go through the gate and enter Mulgrave Woods.

> *This woodland is owned by the Marquis of Normanby who lives in the new Mulgrave Castle. The Mulgrave Estate Woodland is open to access on foot on Saturdays, Sundays and Wednesdays only, but is closed throughout the month of May. Dogs must be on a lead – no exceptions. As these are permissive paths, please respect the wishes of the landowner.*

Pass through the timber yard and go through another gate. Keep on this track through the woods. Keep left at the first fork in the path opposite a small wooden hut on the right.

> *The white flowers of the greater stitchwort can be found in these woods. They are relatively easy to identify by their five petals, which are divided to half way. It is one of the earliest spring flowers, forming large patches of white beneath hedgerows and in woodland margins. It was once supposed to be a remedy for a stitch or sudden pain in the side.*

The path drops slightly and then begins to climb up to the right. At the next fork bear right and follow the path up the steep side of Castle

Rigg amid some wonderful, huge beech and Scots pine trees. At the top of the hill turn left and follow the path to the castle.

Mulgrave Castle is an interesting thirteenth-century stone enclosure fortress, protected by a massive curtain wall supported by huge buttresses. It was constructed c.1214 and has been the home of the de Mauley, Bigod and Radcliffe families, plus Edmund Lord Sheffield, who was a veteran of the fighting against the Spanish Armada. The central keep has seen many alterations over the centuries, and the entrance was guarded by twin circular towers that rose above a moat crossed by a drawbridge. The castle was in ruins in 1309, but was rebuilt as a hunting lodge with the addition of large Elizabethan mullioned windows. During the Civil War it was held for the king, and as a result, Parliamentarian troops destroyed it in 1647.

Mulgrave Wood near Sandsend.

Walk round the high castle walls and then turn left down the path just after the imposing entrance towers.

In 1743, the Mulgrave estate was inherited by the Phipps family, who commissioned landscape architect, Humphrey Repton, to 'romanticise' the ruins. It was he who built the entrance towers, but by this time the family were living in the 'new' Mulgrave 'castle'. This country house stands overlooking the sea near Lythe, about a mile north-east of the old ruins.

Follow the track to a crossroads of tracks, and then turn right through a 'cutting' in the crest of the ridge. Follow the right-hand fork to a

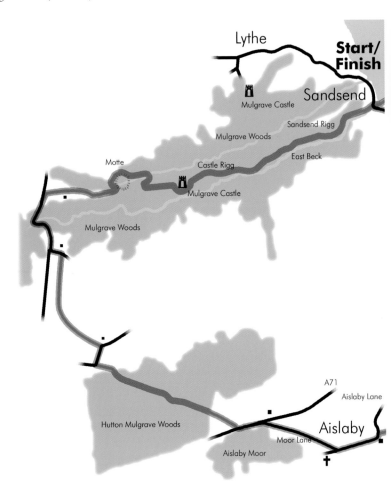

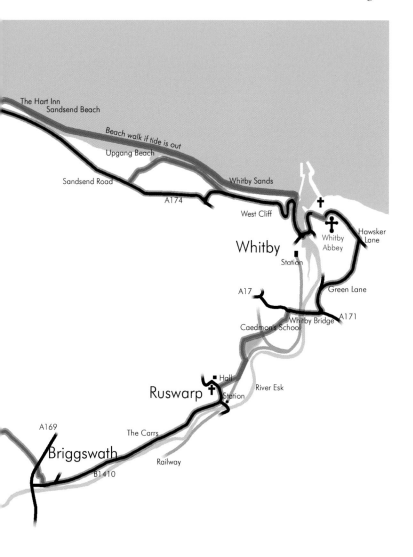

The Hart Inn
Sandsend Beach

Beach walk if tide is out

Upgang Beach

Sandsend Road

A174

Whitby Sands

West Cliff

Whitby

Station

Whitby Abbey

Hawsker Lane

Green Lane

A17

Whitby Bridge

A171

Caedmon's School

Hall

River Esk

Ruswarp

Station

A169

The Carrs

Briggswath

Railway

B1410

Mulgrave Castle.

bridge over the stream and then climb up the other side to a marker post. Turn left along the track and, as it begins to climb, go up the banking on the left in the centre of the hairpin bend. A short distance ahead is a path. Follow this left and then right as it leads through the trees to the motte.

> *Lythe motte is an earthwork motte and bailey fortress, the predecessor of Mulgrave Castle. The large flat motte stands against a deep gorge and the layout of the bailey, with a small barbican to one side, can still be traced. The site is covered in trees and so is best viewed in winter. Such earthworks were often temporary structures, topped with wooden forts and surrounded by a ditch and wooden palisades. When the decision to build a more permanent castle was made, a new site was chosen along Castle Rigg.*

Walk down the moat ditch on the right-hand side of the bluebell-covered motte and then turn right to a gate. Go through the gate and turn left down the lane to the ford through the beck.

Just to the right is a weir, and the remains of buildings almost hidden from view by dense undergrowth indicate that a mill once stood here.

Cross the stream and walk up the track to climb a stile. Follow the fence along the top of the woods to another stile. Climb into a wide green lane and turn right all the way to Barnby Sleights Farm. Go through the gate and continue ahead down the lane to the road.

Barnby Sleights is a name derived from the Old Scandinavian barn-by, the 'farmstead of the children' (i.e. bairns) on the sleights, or 'level fields'. This implies that the farm was probably held by a number of heirs (partible inheritance), rather than through a system of primogeniture, i.e. going to the firstborn.

Turn left at the road, go down over the ford and then back up the other side to a lane on the left, signposted to Epsyke Farm. Opposite Birk Head Farm, turn right into the field and follow the rutted track up the hill with the hedge on the right.

Lythe motte in Mulgrave Wood.

This path is classed as an 'other route with public access' on the OS map. Half way up the hill a large number of holes in the banking over the fence on the right indicate the presence of a thriving badger sett.

Follow the hedge line all the way up the hill as it sweeps round to the left, passing through several gates on the way to Allerton Head Farm. At the farm turn right up the road and over the brow of the hill. After a short distance, take the stile beside the gates on the left and walk up into Hutton Mulgrave Woods.

This is a mixed plantation containing many tree species, including the Turkey oak. It is easily distinguished from Britain's two native oaks, the English oak and the Sessile oak, by its leaves, which are much larger and which have pointed 'digits'. The Turkey oak is a wide-crowned tree with long raised branches, deeply-lobed leaves and mossy-cupped acorns. It was introduced into Britain from the Balkans in 1735.

Follow the muddy forestry track all the way up through the centre of the woods keeping straight ahead past the wireless mast and then down over gorse heathland to reach the main A171 road.

Egton Bridge is two miles down the road to the right. The village plays host to the famous Annual Gooseberry Show, held in the School Hall on the first Tuesday of August each year. It is the oldest gooseberry show in the country, founded in 1800 when an estimated 72 varieties were being grown in Britain. In 1952, Tom Ventress became the World Champion gooseberry grower with a white berry the size of an egg weighing almost 2 ounces.

Turn left down the road and then right, and follow Moor Lane all the way down the hill as its wings left into the village of Aislaby.

Just before the junction, in a field to the right, is Bolton Well, which can be reached by following a cart track from the Aislaby to Egton road. It is possible that the name is linked to the Norse god, Baldur.

Walk past the Huntsman pub and the interesting garden of Pond House, with its intriguing bridge. The main road leaves the village and

Raised paved track, Aislaby.

turns sharply to the left. Go straight ahead down a track, with a raised pavement on the right-hand side. This is Featherbed Lane.

This is a perfect example of an old packhorse route with a paved area to enable pedestrians to pass without getting their feet wet, whilst pack animals and carts would plough through the mud in the main part of the lane. The advantage of using stone slabs can easily be seen – where no slabs were in place the road has eroded away and is now several feet below its original level.

Keep to the paved section of the path – slippery when wet – and follow it to where it turns off down to the right after the mast. The paved path narrows as it descends all the way down to the main A169 road. Cross directly over the main road and walk up the lane opposite, where the paving is resumed once more. Continue to follow the paved path as it winds behind the houses down into the village of Briggswath.

Ruswarp Mill.

Briggswath is a settlement that grew up where the brig or bridge crossed the wath or ford over the river Esk. On the high moors across the river above the village there once stood a Second World War radar station that tracked incoming enemy planes. Indeed, it was this radar that enabled Group Captain Peter Townsend to locate and shoot down the first enemy aircraft of the war over the neighbouring village of Sleights.

Turn left along the road (B1410) all the way to Ruswarp with the River Esk over the field on the right. At Ruswarp the river widens into a 'lake' above the weir that once fed the old mill.

Boating now takes place in Ruswarp (silted land, hris, overgrown by brushwood, wearp) here, amid the swan and mallard, heron can be seen fishing on the far bank. Beside the millpond is the old school, 'erected for the benefit of the poor' by John Elgie in 1848.

Walk to the junction and turn left, 'to Whitby'. Go up the high street with the Church of St Bartholomew on the left, and then take the narrow footpath just before the Old Hall Hotel, signposted 'Whitby 1 mile'.

The mill in Ruswarp by the pond was built for Nathaniel Cholmley of Whitby in 1752. However, the old building was burnt out in 1911 and rebuilt.

Follow this 'pavement' out into fields with a high wall on the right. Go through a couple of stiles, and continue to follow this path, as it swings left towards a wooded hill. Go up the steps and keep on the stone flags to a bench at the top of the hill.

One of the best-loved and most familiar of England's wild flowers is the primrose, from the Latin prima rosa *('first rose'). It is common on well-drained soils in open woodland, scrub, old pastures, churchyards and railway cuttings.*

Turn right and follow the top of the wood to another stile. Turn right and, with allotments on the left, aim for a gate that leads to some steep steps. Drop down into the cutting and climb straight back up the other side. The path now leads out onto the playing fields of Caedmon's School.

Caedmon was the first English poet, and he is commemorated with a cross in the churchyard of St Mary's, which was erected in 1898. The sandstone cross is decorated in Celtic designs with the figures of Christ, David, Abbess Hilda and Caedmon on the side panels.

A 'leaping salmon' signpost indicates which direction to follow. Aim for the right-hand end of the school buildings.

The 'leaping salmon' signs indicate the route of the Esk Valley Walk which follows the River Esk from its source high on the North York Moors to the coast at Whitby, taking walkers from open moorland to farmland pastures.

Go through the gap and walk down the drive to the road. Turn right and cross the high bridge over the River Esk.

This is Whitby Bridge and was opened on 28 March 1980 by the Marquis of Normanby, Her Majesty's Lord Lieutenant of North Yorkshire. The Marquis lives in the latest manifestation of Mulgrave Castle near Sandsend. There are wonderful views from here over Whitby harbour and to the church and abbey on the cliffs above.

Once over the bridge, turn left down the road signposted to Whitby Abbey. Follow the road down to Spittal Bridge and then turn right, up

Whitby Abbey.

Green Lane. Climb this steep hill all the way to the T-junction at the top. Turn left and the abbey is directly ahead.

Whitby Abbey was founded in 657AD, by the Benedictine Order for both men and women. Its founder, St Hild, Abbess of Hartlepool, presided over the Synod of Whitby in 664, at which the country's religious leaders decided to follow the rules of the Roman church rather than those of the Celtic church. The Abbey was subject to Viking raids in 867 and German bombardment in 1914. It was rebuilt and extended over the centuries, until the Dissolution of the Monasteries after which it passed to the Cholmley family. North of the transept is St Hilda's Well or Norman Well, the only survivor of many that once served the abbey.

Follow the path all the way round the abbey wall, signposted 'Headland, St Mary's Church, Town via 199 steps'.

The parish church of St Mary's originates from about 1110, and contains many interesting and unusual features. It is basically a Norman church with Georgian windows, elaborate family pews, a small stove in the nave to warm worshippers, a three-decker pulpit of 1778, galleries everywhere, a bishop's throne of 1778 with high canopy, and one of the most complete sets of Victorian furniture to be seen anywhere. Unlike many churches in the country, this church was never gutted and 'restored' during the Victorian era. It can seat 2,000.

Go through the churchyard and then take the famous 199 steps down into the old town.

When Daniel Defoe visited the town in the early seventeenth century, he noted, 'At the entrance of a little nameless river, scarce indeed worth a name, stands Whitby, which is an excellent harbour and where they build very good ships for the coal trade, which makes the town rich.'

Go ahead and then turn left down the narrow cobbled and pedestrianised streets to the road. Turn right and cross the harbour bridge.

Over the swing-bridge in Church Street is the White Horse and

The Grand Turk, Whitby harbour.

Griffin, built in 1861, which was once a popular meeting place for master mariners and the local gentry, who met for both business and pleasure. Charles Dickens once stayed here.

Turn right and walk all the way to the West Pier. If the tide is out it is possible to walk all the way to Sandsend on the beach, three miles up the coast. However, if the tide is in, it is still possible to walk halfway to Sandsend on the raised sea wall. At the gulley, turn left up the track to the road and follow the road down to Sandsend.

Sandsend is aptly named, sitting at the end of 2½ miles of golden sands, which stretch from Whitby's West Pier to the cliffs of Sandsend Ness.

If the tide is really high it may be safer to climb the winding road up to the whalebone arch and Captain Cook's monument at West Cliff and follow the road along the clifftops all the way back into Sandsend.

The monument to Captain Cook on the West Cliff was unveiled in 1923. It was from Whitby that Cook first went to sea and

where his most famous ship, Endeavour, *was built in 1765. Nearby is the famous whalebone arch, signifying the importance of the whaling industry to this busy port during the eighteenth and early nineteenth centuries.*

Where East Beck enters the sea, the road turns inland and the pub is just around the corner.

Captain Cook and the whalebone arch.

Castle Bolton
and Nappa Hall

28.5 km/18.5 miles

Explorer OL30 *Yorkshire Dales Northern
and Central areas*

Start from the Wheatsheaf in Carperby

*The Wheatsheaf is famed as the inn where vet James
Herriot stayed on his honeymoon in 1941. Carperby
(the farmstead of a man called Cairpre) stands on the
high escarpment above the River Ure in the centre of
Wensleydale. Cairpre is an Old Irish personal name
and '-by' a Viking word for a farmstead, so the
foundersof this settlement were possibly of
mixed Irish/Viking origin.*

Turn right out of the pub and walk up to the village green, taking the
street round to the right of the dated cross of 1674. Follow the street
past the old school and Wesleyan chapel and then turn right at the
far end of the village past West End Farm. Go through two gates and
then keep directly ahead though the farmyard and up the hill,
climbing two yellow-painted stone stiles on the way.

*Working farm dogs are a necessity of the countryside for
herding livestock and acting as very effective guard dogs when
firmly chained to their kennels in farmyards. Border collies, in
particular, are excellent for working sheep due to their high
intelligence and tireless energy. A tax on keeping dogs was
levied between 1796 and 1882, depending on the type of dog.
House dogs, i.e. pets, were levied at a lower rate than sporting
dogs, and packs of hounds were charged per pack. Working
dogs (sheepdogs) were exempt.*

177

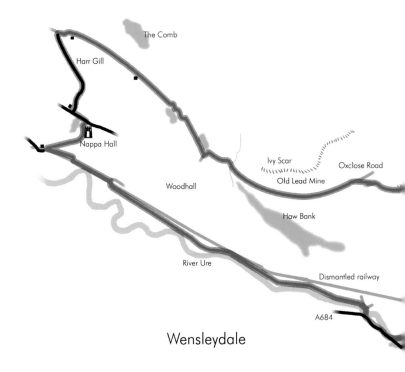

The Comb

Harr Gill

Nappa Hall

Ivy Scar

Oxclose Road

Old Lead Mine

Woodhall

Haw Bank

River Ure

Dismantled railway

A684

Wensleydale

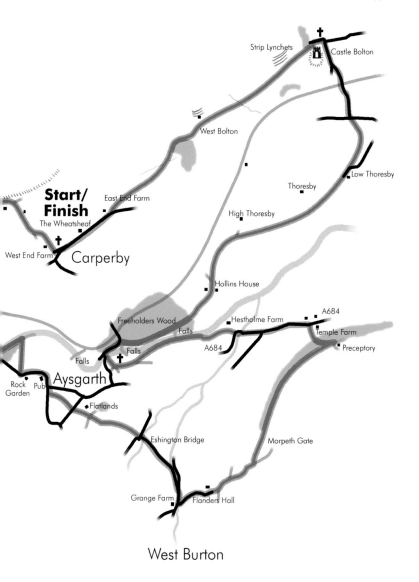

Strip Lynchets

Castle Bolton

West Bolton

Low Thoresby

Thoresby

**Start/
Finish**

East End Farm

High Thoresby

The Wheatsheaf

West End Farm

Carperby

Hollins House

Hestholme Farm

A684

Freeholders Wood

Temple Farm

Falls

Preceptory

Falls

A684

Falls

Aysgarth

Rock
Garden

Pub

Flatlands

Eshington Bridge

Morpeth Gate

Grange Farm

Flanders Hall

West Burton

After the second stile, veer over to a stile on the left and turn right to follow the track up the hill past the barn.

Issuing from the limestone scar up to the right is Kendalacre Well, which falls into a trough and forms a rocky stream.

Go through the gate at the very top of the field, turn right briefly, and then go left up another track, which leads into the quarry workings of Ponderledge Scar.

There are panoramic views up and down Wensleydale, characterised by the many stone barns that stand in virtually every field.

Follow the track through a gate and round to the right following the far wall. Where the way is blocked by a steep bank turn left through the gateway. Cut up the bank on the right and head out into the middle of the field to join a wide green path, called Ox Close Road.

The name 'Ox Close' alludes to the importance of the ox as a draught animal until recent times. The moors here are covered in yellow mountain pansy and the occasional early purple orchid. There is nothing more wonderful than suddenly coming upon a beautiful flower. Found on grassy pastures and hedge banks, the early purple orchid is an erect perennial rising from two egg-shaped tubers. (The name orchid comes from orchis, *the Greek for testicle.) The tubers can be gathered and made into a healthy milky drink, being gentle on the stomach and full of minerals. Orchids are not that common in Britain and it is illegal to dig them up, as is the case with many wild flowers.*

Turn left through the gate and continue across the moor on this pleasant green path, gradually dropping towards an old lead mine, under the shadow of Ivy Scar.

Haw Bank, or Wet Grooves, lead mine is thought to date from 1765. Groove or grove is an old term for a mine used as far back as the sixteenth century. The name of this mine suggests that it was susceptible to flooding. Lead had been mined in Yorkshire since the Bronze Age, although the 'golden age' was during the great castle and cathedral building campaigns of

View along the escarpment above Wensleydale.

the twelfth century onwards. It is said that lead from Yorkshire mines was used on Windsor Castle, on St Peter's in Rome and even on church roofs in Jerusalem. During this time, much of the county's lead production was dominated by the monasteries, who ran the mines. Lead was used for roofs, pipes, cisterns and guttering, and those who worked in lead were called 'plumbers', derived from the Latin for lead. Mining experienced a further resurgence during the Industrial Revolution.

The path passes to the left of the old lead mine, where it becomes a gravel track. Follow the track through a gate and through a stream, and on up the hillside. Where the walled lane ends, turn left through a gateway and walk the short distance ahead to a signpost.

The famous Wensleydale cheese is made further up the valley in the market town of Hawes. It is said that cheese making was brought to Wensleydale by French monks who settled near Aysgarth in 1145. After the Dissolution of the Monasteries in the reign of Henry VIII, cheese-making skills passed into the hands of local farmers and were eventually inherited by the present factory at Hawes in the nineteenth century.

Turn right and follow the signs to Askrigg, up the hill passing through the gates and fields all the way to the right-hand edge of a small copse. Go through the gate and keep the boundary wall on the left. Follow this wall along the hillside to a stone barn. Go through the gate on the right and follow the walled lane to its junction with the narrow road. Turn left and walk down the steep hill, Harr Gill.

Half way down the hill there are expansive views to the west. Of particular note is a perfectly straight Roman road running all the way down from the summit of Wether Fell (a 'wether' is a castrated ram) to the Roman fort at Bainbridge, called Virosidum. Down to the left of the road is Baydale, within which is Semerwater, the only natural lake in Yorkshire.

At the main road turn left. Walk a short distance along the road, and cross over to go through the gate marked 'Nappa Hall'. Walk down the farm track and through the farmyard buildings with Nappa Hall on the left.

In the early fifteenth century, Thomas Metcalf bought a cottage on this site from the Lords Scrope of Castle Bolton. However, to defend his family and livestock against Scottish raids, he added pele towers and additional wings, plus a fortified curtain wall. The Nappa Hall of today dates from 1459, and was the Metcalfs' home for many generations. The Metcalfs were minor gentry, acting as estate stewards for the abbots of Jervaulx and king's wardens of the Forest of Wensleydale. They became very powerful, with Sir Christopher Metcalf elected to High Sheriff of Yorkshire. When the Judge of the Assizes met in York, Metcalf arrived at the head of 300 Metcalfs, all mounted on white horses. By the end of the Middle Ages, the Metcalfs were the largest family in England. Mary Queen of Scots was once imprisoned in the house, possibly before she was moved to Castle Bolton further down the dale, and her ghost is said to haunt the hall.

At the bottom of the lane take the last gate on the right and walk out across the field aiming for a telegraph pole. Continue into the next field and drop down towards the barn in the far corner. Just before the barn go through the gate and turn left, as indicated by a sign to 'Woodhall and Aysgarth'.

Nappa Hall.

The fortified peel or pele towers of Nappa Hall take their name from the Old French piel *meaning 'stake', originally being a fence of stakes or a defensive wall. The name Nappa is most likely derived from enclosure* haeg *in a bowl-shaped hollow* hnaepp, *as in* hnaepp-haeg.

Walk along the bottom of the two fields with the line of the old railway on the immediate right.

The first sections of the Wensleydale railway were opened in 1848 to provide a 40-mile link for passengers and goods between Northallerton, on the east coast main line, and the Settle–Carlisle line in the west. From the 1950s, these services were gradually withdrawn, until, in 1964, only the Northallerton to Redmire section remained for goods traffic. However, in 1992 all traffic stopped completely, although the track was still in place.

A stile soon leads up the bank onto the embankment on the right.

Hilltop copse, Woodhall Park.

Follow this until a fence bars the way where a sign indicates a metal kissing gate on the right. Go through the gate and turn left to follow the base of the embankment along the flood plain, with the River Ure meandering along the lush valley over to the right. The path now follows the river all the way back to Aysgarth, between the embankment on the left and the river on the right. Keep going straight on at all times.

The flood debris in the trees at head height indicates that the river is susceptible to flooding. At such times, it may be prudent to seek refuge on the railway embankment.

At Woodhall Park the path is bounded by a high stone wall on the left. Go straight ahead and stay by the river, eventually reaching a stile that leads out onto a lane. Walk ahead for a short distance, and then turn right down the tarmac path that leads to the footbridge over the river.

The River Ure is one of the larger rivers draining off the eastern flanks of the Pennines, its source being high on the moors of Mallerstang Common. The wide, open landscape of Wensleydale is due to glacial erosion where deposits have been reworked by the river into a series of river terraces. The river meanders over the flat valley floor as it passes east through Bainbridge, Aysgarth and Wensley, at which point it leaves the Pennines and flows through the Vale of York.

Turn left at the road, and then take the footpath on the left to follow the riverbank through a field and into woods. The path slowly begins to climb the banking and leads to a ladder stile that climbs out into a field. Turn left and walk past the barn to a lane. Turn right and walk all the way up into the village. Turn left towards the village green.

Across the road at this point is the Aysgarth Edwardian Rock Garden. It was built between 1906 and 1914 for alpine enthusiast and amateur horticulturalist, Frank Sayer Graham. This colourful character collected rare sea gulls' eggs and dealt in silver rabbit furs, raised on nearby Lady Hill.

Follow the road through the village and round the corner to the right, on which stands the George and Dragon public house. Walk straight ahead and keep going up the side road, past the petrol station and garage, signposted 'Thoralby'.

A field on the right is called 'Poor's Land', and refers to a plot of land held by the parish on behalf of the poor who were allowed to cut furze (gorse) there for fuel or graze any stock they may have had.

Opposite the last house on the right, take the stile into the field on the left. The path goes across the bottom of the field to another stile and then cuts the right-hand corner off the next field. Go straight through the centre of the next field to the road.

Aysgarth (open place where oak trees grow) is a pretty little village sitting high on the bank above the river, at a point just before it narrows and cascades over a series of wide waterfalls.

Turn left for a short distance and take the stile on the right, signposted 'Eshington Bridge ½ mile'. Walk forward aiming for the lowest part of this field in the dip. Drop down the green gulley and cross through the fence at the crossroad of footpaths.

Swaledale sheep are common in this area, being easily distinguished by their curly 'permed' wool.

Go up the opposite bank and then take the stile on the left through the wall. Turn right and walk diagonally down the next field towards the bottom left-hand corner. Go through the gate, turn right and walk

View across Bishopdale.

all the way down the hill to the road. Walk ahead down the road and over Eshington Bridge.

The bridge crosses Bishopdale Beck flowing out of Bishopdale on its way to join the River Ure near Hestholme Farm. Bishopdale is a classic U-shaped glacial valley, formed by the gouging action of tons of ice. Bishopdale Beck is the largest of the many tributaries that drain into the River Ure in Wensleydale.

Almost immediately, take the stile on the right, and turn left to follow the wall to another stile that leads back out onto the road. Keep on the pavement and walk into West Burton.

West Burton is a picturesque village with a large green, market cross and stocks. An ancient packhorse bridge crosses Walden Beck. The Cauldron Falls are further upstream.

Opposite the first house on the right, Grange Farm Cottage, turn left up the steps and over the narrow packhorse bridge over Walden Beck. Follow the lane past Flanders Hall and up towards the farm. The lane goes round the back of the farm and begins to climb up the hill.

This is Morpeth Gate that becomes High Lane, which was once a busy drove road, taking livestock from Bishopdale to the market in Middleham.

Pass a sign to Temple Farm and look out for the footpath sign on the left to Templars' Chapel. Follow the contours of the hill as the path sweeps round the hillside with Morpeth Wood below and the crags of West Witton Moor above.

The highest point of the moor above is called Penhill, which has an interesting derivation. The Celtic word for 'hill' is pen *as seen in Pen-y-ghent. When the Anglo-Saxons arrived they asked the locals what this particular hill was called and the local population said simply 'pen' (i.e. just a hill), so the Anglo-Saxons, thinking this was a specific name, called it Pen Hill, its name today, which actually means 'hill hill'.*

After climbing a number of gate-stiles and walking through several fields, the path reaches a lane, over which lie the remains of a preceptory of the Knights' Templar.

The name 'preceptory' refers to a subordinate house or community of the Knights Templar. This example was built c.1200, but was handed over to the Hospitallers when the Templars were suppressed in 1312. The chapel was uncovered in 1840, and stands amid other buildings as yet unexcavated.

Turn left and walk down the rocky lane into the wood. Follow the path round to the right and down to the road beside Temple Farm.

Remains of the Knights Templar preceptory.

187

The Order of the Knights Templar was founded in Jerusalem in 1119, to protect European pilgrims on their travels through the Holy Land. By 1150, this military/religious order had extended its operations throughout Christendom, including England, where they acquired land at Penhill and built this chapel dedicated to 'God, the Virgin and St Catherine'. However, the order became too wealthy and too powerful, and members were charged with using illegal means to acquire property and wealth, acts of sodomy, worshipping idols, and committing obscene and sacrilegious acts on the cross and on the image of Christ. In 1312, Pope Clement V abolished the order and most of the Templars were imprisoned, tortured and executed.

Turn left and walk down the road and over the bridge over Walden Beck.

Just before the bridge stands a well-kept old AA telephone box from the days when other 'knights of the road' attended to travellers in trouble!

As the road swings to the left, take the footpath on the right at the top of the drive to Hestholme Farm. Walk diagonally across the field to a large beech tree beside the wooded riverbank and turn left. Follow the river upstream passing through a number of gate-stiles.

Signs advise, 'Please keep your dog on a lead. The landowner has had great problems with dogs in the past.' Please respect the landowner's wishes. The riverbanks are covered in flowers, including cowslip and the early purple orchid.

After the third stile, the path leads up the bank on the left, still following the river, but now from atop the high bank, passing a marker post on the way. Go through a gate-stile behind the large holly tree and then up the wooden steps. Go over the brow of the hill beside the remains of an old stone wall.

Different areas have different styles of stiles, depending on materials available and on building tradition. In Wensleydale, gated stiles are the norm, whereby a small wooden gate is set above the stile at such an angle that it will close by gravitational pull. They are fittingly known as 'bastard stiles'.

Head for the left-hand side of the small copse. Go through the wood and then head for the gate into the churchyard.

St Andrew's Church has a fourteenth-century bell tower, although the body of the church was rebuilt in 1866. When Henry VIII dissolved the monasteries in 1536, after being excommunicated by Pope Paul III, several items, including the finely carved rood screen and the abbot's stall, were removed from Jervaulx Abbey and installed in the church. During the twelfth century, Aysgarth was the largest parish in England, covering some 81,000 acres in Upper Wensleydale.

Walk up past the church and turn right round the tower to a metal gate. Walk down the steps to come out on the road beside the old mill.

Aysgarth is also the home of the Yorkshire Carriage Museum, housed in a former cotton mill. After a fire in 1853 it was rebuilt and re-equipped for the spinning of wool. The mill was responsible for supplying the material that clothed Garibaldi's red-shirts during the Italian revolution of the mid-nineteenth century.

Go straight ahead over the road bridge and follow the road round to the right. Walk up the road to where it swings round to the left.

The original single-arch bridge over the river at Aysgarth mill was built in 1539, but has been widened more recently. It is possible to get a good view of the older span from below.

Take the footpath on the right into Freeholder's Wood Nature Reserve and follow the path down to the right, keeping ahead through the wood.

At Aysgarth, the River Ure plunges 200 feet in less than a mile over three spectacular waterfalls. Take time out to view the Middle and Lower Falls as indicated. It was here at Aysgarth that the Robin Hood/Little John river fight scene for Kevin Costner's Robin Hood: Prince of Thieves *was filmed.*

The path leads out into Riddings Field, past a highly carved seat, inscribed 'Ancient pasture filled with flowers, sheep and cattle enrich

Aysgarth Falls.

the soil'. Just after the seat a sign on the left to Castle Bolton and Redmire indicates where to leave the main path. Walk across the grass on the left towards the fence, and then follow the fence along to the right.

'Riddings' is a term associated with the clearance of trees. Over the fence on the left is St Joseph's Wood, a Millennium Project plantation and nature reserve.

Follow the path to a stile and climb out into a field. Aim for a gate at the lower end of Hollins House Farm. Follow the track into the farmyard and then walk past the house to follow the lane up the hill. At the sign, turn right and go through the left-hand of two field gates. The path leads to a stile-gate and into a large meadow.

Walkers are advised that this is 'meadowland for winter feed, so please keep in single file'. Depending upon the time of year, this field, like many others, can be filled with the much-maligned dandelion. These common plants, of which there are many varieties, form the familiar seed 'clock' much loved by children of all ages. It can, of course, also be combined with another plant, burdock, to make a popular soft drink.

Walk directly over the meadow, with High Thoresby Farm in the foreground and the impressive ruins of Castle Bolton on the hillside beyond.

The name of Thoresby ('Thor's settlement') is yet another indication that this upland region was colonised by

Scandinavian farmers from Denmark during the ninth and tenth centuries, when much of the eastern half of England made up the kingdom of the Danelaw.

At the end of the field, turn right and follow the sign to Castle Bolton along the wall. Climb a stile and go through a gate, with a wall now on the right, until the signpost is reached. Follow the direction indicated to cut the corner of the field off, rejoining the boundary wall after a short distance. Keep the wall on the immediate right to a gate. Climb the stile ahead and walk down the somewhat overgrown footpath (Thoresby Lane) all the way to Low Thoresby.

On the moors above the castle can be seen a large chimney, a solitary reminder of the mining that once took place between Bolton and Grinton.

Walk past the farm to where the tarmac lane begins. Almost immediately, turn left up the bank and over the stile. Walk ahead through a broken down stone wall, and turn right. Walk up the meadow to the far right-hand corner. Climb the stile and follow the path through another meadow to the road.

These traditional meadows are a sea of colour in the summer with many different flowers, including the multi-flowered white woodruff and the pink water avens, with its demure-looking, nodding, bell shaped flowers. The water avens is common in the

Dales barns, Wensleydale.

wetter north of Britain, and is to be found by streams and damp, shady places, including woodlands. The pink flowers, which often hang down like nodding bells, are pollinated by bumblebees. It is closely related to the smaller yellow wood avens, which is found in open woodland and hedgerows.

Cross the road and climb the hill up to Castle Bolton (½ mile), crossing the line of the old Wensleydale railway on the way.

As the track was never removed when the line closed in 1992, the Wensleydale Railway Company decided to re-open sections of the line in July 2003. The company launched the first scheduled passenger services to be seen on this line for nearly 50 years, and there were scenes of jubilation as the first trains rolled out of Leeming Bar and Leyburn stations. This hailed the start of greater things for the local community and for leisure and tourism along the line, and it is hoped that the service may one day be extended to Bolton Abbey, Aysgarth and beyond . . .

At the top of the hill turn left between the imposing ruins of Castle Bolton and fourteenth-century St Oswald's Church.

Castle Bolton (settlement with a special building) is made up of houses lining either side of a single, wide street that leads up to the castle gates. In 1530, Leland described it as 'a very rough place, but its castle, which is not a large building and is all compressed within four or five towers, has an attractive park next to it.' The church was built around 1325, and is dedicated to St Oswald, the seventh-century king and martyr. A sundial on the buttress east of the porch implies that it was built before being overshadowed by the castle.

Walk past the castle and through a gate onto the lane beside the car park.

Castle Bolton was finished in 1399, having taken Sir Richard le Scrope, former Lord Chancellor to Richard II, eighteen years to build. The Scrope family is mentioned in three of Shakespeare's plays – Richard II, Henry IV and Henry V – and was involved in most political events throughout the fourteenth to seventeenth centuries. Queen Elizabeth I imprisoned Mary Queen of Scots here in 1568, under the care of Sir Francis Knollys, and during the British Civil War it was besieged by surrounded Parliamentarian troops, holding out for one year in 1644–45, until the garrison was starved out. The castle is a formidable, square, four-towered structure around an enclosed courtyard that dominates Wensleydale to this day. Pevsner describes it as 'a climax of English military architecture'.

Go through the field gate and then veer off the lane towards the bottom end of the small copse. Go through the wood to come out in a large field. Head out past the wall and keep ahead across the field, aiming for a field gate in the far fence.

The fields around Castle Bolton are characterised by strip lynchets. Strip lynchets are long terraced fields laid out on sloping ground in the post-Roman and medieval periods. These fields are home to the lapwing, and these noisy 'peewits' will often 'dive bomb' walkers during the nesting season.

Walk across the next field aiming for a line of telegraph poles and follow these to the wall on the right. Go through the stile and walk down into the gulley to cross Beldon Beck by a small footbridge. Walk up the far bank to a stile on the right. Follow the wall ahead, aiming directly for the front of the farmhouse.

Farmers in environmentally important areas like the Yorkshire Dales are being encouraged to turn to more traditional methods of agriculture and husbandry by farming more traditional breeds of livestock. One of the hardiest breeds of cattle is the Dexter, which originally comes from Ireland but which is ideally suited to the upland pastures of the Dales. They are small and can stay out all winter and, when reared properly, produce possibly the best beef available anywhere.

Go round the left-hand side of the farm and through the farmyard. Just after the last building, turn right into the field and walk around the wood, West Bolton Plantation, to a gate. Drop down the slope and cross the marshy stream using the remains of an old stone wall as stepping stones. Turn right and follow the stream to a stile in the wall. Walk ahead up the next two fields passing a barn on the way

Castle Bolton.

to a muddy track that becomes a lane leading down to East End Farm.

Many of the fields in this area are carpeted with buttercups. The meadow buttercup was once one of Britain's most common and well-loved flowers. However, modern farming methods and the preference for plain green 'Euro-grass' instead of flower-filled meadows has seen their numbers decline. The whole plant is poisonous and so is avoided by grazing animals, although they are safe if dried within hay. The acrid sap can blister the mouth and skin. If a buttercup is held beneath the chin and the skin shines yellow it is supposed to mean that the person likes butter!

Just before the farm, turn left through a stile and over a muddy stream, and follow the wall to the road. Turn right at the road and walk the short distance back to the Wheatsheaf.

Carlton Motte, William's Hill and Middleham Castle

20.5 km/13 miles

Explorer OL30 *Yorkshire Dales Northern and Central areas*

Start at the Three Horseshoes in Wensley

The small village of Wensley is unique in that it gives its name to this famous dale, whereas the others all take their names from the rivers that flow through them. In Anglo-Saxon times Wensley village was called Woden's lea and is thought to have been the site of a pagan shrine. However, in the sixteenth century, Leland referred to this 'poor market town' as 'Vensela' and the inhabitants as 'Vennones'.

Walk down the road, passing the entrance to Bolton Hall on the right and the church on the left.

Holy Trinity Church was built in 1245 and contains the arms of George III and those of the Scrope family (of Castle Bolton). The Scrope's private pew, of the later seventeenth century, came at a time when chantries were being abolished. An early wall painting, dating from c.1330, is just one of many treasures in this unspoiled church.

Cross the bridge and go through the gate on the immediate right.

Wensleydale's river is the Ure, an old Celtic river name related to the Gaulish river name Isura. The bridge has four arches, one of which is pointed. In 1530, John Leland recorded that, 'there

The entrance to Bolton Hall, Wensley.

*is a fine bridge of three or four arches across the Ure at
Wensley ... it was built over two hundred years ago by the
parson of Wensley whose name was Alwyn', making it a
fourteenth-century construction – if this is the same bridge.*

Walk ahead through the wood beside the river until eventually
climbing the bank on the left. Cross the field to a gate and turn right,
up the lane to the road.

*Back down the lane is Lord's Bridge that leads over the Ure to
Bolton Hall, home of Lord Bolton. Bolton Hall is the family seat
of the Orde Powlett family, and was built by the Marquis of
Winchelsea, first Duke of Bolton, in 1678. It was burned out in
1902, after which it was extensively repaired.*

Cross directly over the road (A684) and walk straight up Bay Bolton
Avenue past Park Gate Farm. The route is now going to go in a straight
line from the river to the top of Capple Bank. At the end of the
avenue, the track turns left, but keep ahead over a stile into the
wooded hillside. Keep straight ahead up the hill, crossing a track
halfway up.

*This small fir plantation is carpeted with bluebell and white-
flowered ramsons at certain times of the year. The leaves of*

ramsons are edible and can smell very strongly of garlic, a defence against insects and other predators.

At the top edge of the wood, climb the stile and turn left briefly, to go through the gateway. Walk ahead through another gateway in the fence and skirt around to the left of the small scar.

A folly tower is clearly visible over to the left in Mount Park.

Strike out straight across the field, on the same heading as when climbing up the hill, until reaching the wooded Capple Bank. Climb the stile into the wood and follow the steps up the steep bank to come out on the road. Turn right.

On the left at this point are the Gallops where racehorses are trained. Nearby Middleham is home to several prestigious racehorse stables, and has been for many years. In 1911, the young George Formby, a thin, sickly lad, was sent to work at Lord Derby's stables in Middleham. He made a poor jockey but in 1915 he appeared as a jockey in an unmemorable film called By the shortest of heads. *After the war, during which time George worked at the Curragh in Ireland, he returned to Middleham once more and remained there until 1920.*

Walk ahead to Penhill Farm then turn left up the road signposted to Melmerby and Carlton. Once over the cattle grid, leave the road and

Field barn near Bolton Bridge.

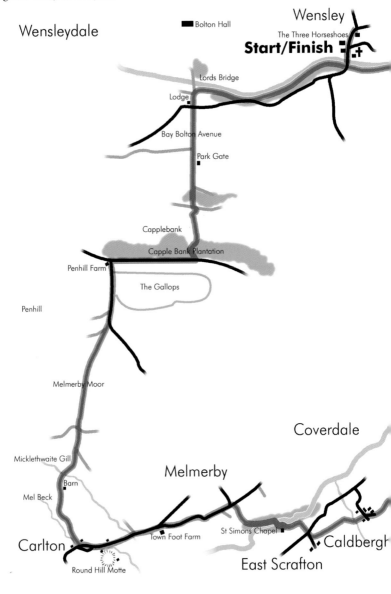

Wensleydale

Bolton Hall

Wensley

The Three Horseshoes
Start/Finish

Lords Bridge

Lodge

Bay Bolton Avenue

Park Gate

Capplebank

Capple Bank Plantation

Penhill Farm

The Gallops

Penhill

Melmerby Moor

Coverdale

Micklethwaite Gill

Barn

Melmerby

Mel Beck

Town Foot Farm

St Simons Chapel

Caldbergh

Carlton

Round Hill Motte

East Scrafton

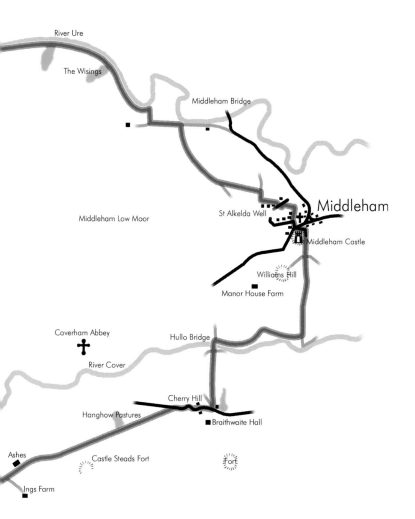

River Ure

The Wisings

Middleham Bridge

Middleham Low Moor

St Alkelda Well

Middleham

Middleham Castle

Williams Hill

Manor House Farm

Coverham Abbey

River Cover

Hullo Bridge

Cherry Hill

Hanghow Pastures

Braithwaite Hall

Ashes

Castle Steads Fort

Fort

Ings Farm

go straight ahead up the track onto the moor. After a short distance, the path crosses a wide track that leads to Penhill.

> *'Penhill' has an interesting derivation. The Celtic word for 'hill' is* pen *as seen in Pen-y-ghent and many Welsh place-names. When the Anglo-Saxons arrived in England they took the Celtic word for hill as being its specific name, and thereafter called it Pen Hill, which simply means 'hill hill'. On the slopes of Penhill is Robin Hood's Well, a natural spring that soon forms a rushing stream.*

Keep straight ahead over Melmerby Moor, following the track over the heather until it begins to descend to meet a farm track. Cross the track and go over a small bridge and through the gate. Walk down the field to another gate and then turn right and walk directly ahead to cross a narrow steep-sided gulley, aiming for the barn.

> *Micklethwaite Gill comes from* mickle, *or large, and* thwaite, *or clearing, in a wooded valley or* gill.

Cross the stream and then go through the gate to the right of the barn. Follow the track to the bottom of the field, and then turn left down into the village of Carlton.

> *One house (up the road to the right) has a three-bay front with flat mullioned windows and an interesting inscription to Henry Constantine, the 'Coverdale Bard', dated 1861.*

Turn left and walk down the main street past the Foresters' Arms behind which is Round Hill motte.

> *Carlton is a very common name in the old Danelaw areas of north England, meaning a settlement or* tun *of the freemen or peasants,* ceorl. *The motte lies down a farm track beyond the stream. The flat-topped mound is very pronounced but the bailey has been subsumed by the farm buildings. It was possibly an outpost of Middleham Castle, built to keep watch up the upper valley. On the other side of the road behind the houses the fields are called Poor's Land, indicating land once held by the Parish Council for use by the poor.*

Walk out of the village, passing two left-hand junctions signposted to

Carlton motte.

Melmerby. Just after the second junction, take the footpath on the right, signposted 'East Scrafton ¾'. Walk down a wide green lane lined with mature ash trees to the field, and then turn left and walk to a stile in the far corner of the field.

It is hard to imagine now but the small village of Carlton lies on the once strategic coaching route that linked the castles of Lancaster, Skipton and Middleham. Merchants' packhorses used to pass through the village, as did coaches on the London to Richmond route, when much of the dale was a deer park. The inns were stopping off places where weary horses could be changed and weary travellers refreshed.

Walk ahead through the gateway and keep the fence on the right, high above the River Cover. Follow the fence down the slope to a stile on the right, and then go down the steep winding steps that lead to St Simon's bridge over the river. Go over the footbridge and turn left, crossing a small bridge and a stile along the wooded riverbank to the ruins of St Simon's Chapel.

St Simon's Chapel, Coverdale.

On the banks of the Cover once stood an oratory called St Simon's Chapel, of which only a few moss-covered walls now remain. The chapel was dedicated to St Simon and St Jude, and was first recorded in 1328. It was built as a 'chapel-of-ease', where people could worship without travelling long distances to the parish church at Coverham. By 1582 the chapel was described as ruins but four years later part of it was being used as an alehouse! Nearby is St Simon's Well, formerly used as a bath, and reputed to be beneficial to certain diseases. It issues from stone conduits into what was once a large stone-paved bath.

Pass the chapel and the remains of an old lime kiln on the right, and go up the stone steps to a gate at the top of the bank. Cross the field to the road and go straight over up the lane towards East Scrafton. Just before the high wall, turn left over a stile where a signpost says 'Caldbergh ½ mile'.

Scrafton comes from 'farmstead' tun near a 'hollow' scraef. Old monastic routes once connected the abbeys with their lands in this area and were often marked with stone crosses. A well-used road ran between Jervaulx and its colliery near West Scrafton, where records show that coal was being mined as far back as 1334.

Walk beside the wall and then strike out into the field, following a line of mature sycamore to a section of wall end on. Follow the right-hand side of the wall to a stile into the wood. Cross the small bridge and walk up the far bank.

The sycamore is a large, domed tree with dark green, five-pointed, lobed leaves. The flowers hang in yellow clusters in April, which ripen to pairs of winged fruits that spiral in the wind once released from the tree. It is a member of the maple family.

Turn half right across the field aiming for a small wooden gate in the opposite fence that leads into another wood. The path drops down into the wood, over the stream and then up the far bank beside the wall to lead between farm buildings behind Caldbergh Hall.

Caldbergh (cold hill) is a small hamlet nestling on the valley slopes beneath Caldbergh Moor and the wooded Coverdale below. Miles Coverdale, the English Protestant reformer and biblical scholar, was born in Coverdale in 1488. He studied at Cambridge, was ordained a priest in Norwich, and joined the Augustinians before being converted to Protestantism. In 1535, he published the first translation of the whole Bible in English, dedicated to Henry VIII, and in 1551 he was made Bishop of Exeter, but had to flee when Mary I ascended the throne. He eventually returned to England in 1559 and died in 1568.

Go through the gate and walk down the lane to the road. Turn right and walk up through the gate, where a sign says 'Braithwaite 1½ miles' and 'Unsuitable for motor traffic'. Follow this rough track up and along the hillside, following the contours past Ings and Ashes Farms.

Down the hill on the left as the path approaches Ashes Farm is Bank Hills Well. It is a beautiful natural spring that was probably once a wayside well.

Keep all the way along this track to some sheepfolds.

Half way up the hill to the right is Castle Steads, an Iron Age hill fort, one of a number in this region.

Go through a red gate just after the sheep pen and then follow the wall to a wooden gate, where the fence turns right up the hill. Go through the gate and strike out across the field aiming for the right-hand end of a copse of conifer trees called Hanghow Pastures, climbing a stile on the way.

Down in the valley at this point is a large farm, behind which can be seen all that remains of the Premonstratensian Coverham Abbey, which was founded in 1212 by Ranulphus Fitz-Robert. The Norman gateway is still complete, and two arches of the nave of the abbey church remain. Several inscribed stones are built into the walls of the mansion, one of which states that 'the abbot happily finished this house in 1508', probably a restoration. It is a much-converted site, and now a private residence. The Premonstratensian Order was founded in 1121 by St Norbert at Prémontré near Laon in Northern France, and the monks were called the 'white canons' as they wore white habits and caps.

The path now begins to slowly descend the hillside to a stile in the far bottom corner of the field by the road. Turn right past Cherry Hill Farm and then left down the footpath signposted 'Hullo Bridge ½ mile', opposite the entrance to Braithwaite Hall.

The National Trust manages a network of permissive paths in this area, which allow access along the riverbank and up onto the moors above Braithwaite Hall to visit East Witton Iron Age camps The paths pass through traditional hay meadows and pastures that are farmed less intensively under the Countryside Stewardship Scheme.

Walk straight down through the meadow to a stile in the corner and from there go straight ahead down to cross Hullo Bridge and the River Cover. Take the stile on the right and walk along the bank and then up the path through the trees on the left. Turn right and follow the path along beside the top of the wooded bank.

These lush meadows are often filled with grazing racehorses, while on Middleham Low Moor are more gallops along which the horses are trained. From 1784 to 1874 a tax was levied on the possession of racehorses.

Go over a stile and head for the left-hand end of a small stand of Scots pine. Go through the narrow wood and turn right. Follow the fence all the way down to the right. Just before coming out high above the river turn left to a tall solitary marker post. At the post turn left and follow the wall up the rise. Go over the crest of the hill to a stile.

> *Over to the left at this point is William's Hill, a tree-covered motte, which is the site of the original castle at Middleham. It comprises a ringwork of great strength, a bailey and wet defences, i.e. a moat. The castle here was built c.1070 by Alan the 'Red', Earl of Richmond, who also built Richmond Castle, although it was dismantled in 1170 when the present castle was built. Its eastern approach along the ridge is also defended by a series of banks and ditches, running north to south.*

Keep ahead over the next small rise and then, all of a sudden, Middleham castle appears down the hill ahead.

William's Hill motte above Middleham.

Middleham Castle.

Middleham Castle contains a great Norman keep of the late twelfth century and a curtain wall, towers and gatehouse from the fourteenth and fifteenth centuries. The keep is one of the largest in England, having twelve-foot thick walls and three floors. For extra defence a wide ditch was dug around these walls and access to the castle was by a gatehouse with a drawbridge in the north-east corner.

Go through the gate into the lane. On the left is a small gate from which a path leads up to William's Hill. Return to this point and continue down Canaan Lane beside the castle.

The castle was the home of Richard Neville, the Earl of Warwick, who was known as the 'Kingmaker' for his support of King Edward IV in the Wars of the Roses. From 1465 to 1468 Edward's brother Richard, Duke of Gloucester, the future King Richard III, stayed at Middleham Castle under the care of Warwick. Only a year after Richard had left Middleham, Warwick turned against King Edward and imprisoned the king in the castle. For a few months during Edward's imprisonment, Warwick attempted to rule the country in the king's name, but was slain at the Battle of Barnet in 1471. Richard faired better – he inherited the castle, married Warwick's daughter and was crowned king himself in 1483.

Turn left along the front of the castle to the road and cross between the remains of the market cross and the Queen Victoria Jubilee fountain.

The cross commemorates the granting of a fair and market twice yearly in Middleham (middle homestead ham) in 1479 at the feast of St Simon and St Jude, by Richard Duke of Gloucester, later King Richard III. The heraldic animal is thought to be his emblem, a white boar.

Head down the street that leads off between the fountain and cross, signposted to the church and 'key centre', to the left of the battlemented gallery that was once a school of 1869. Pass the Methodist chapel and take the footpath on the right where the road turns to the left, and walk down to the church. Turn left in the churchyard to a gate.

Middleham Church is dedicated to St Mary and St Alkelda and, traditionally, the building was erected adjoining St Alkelda's Well, after this pious lady was murdered there in 800AD. Her shrine in the church attracted pilgrims until the Reformation and is marked by a Saxon carving, thought to be part of her tomb. The bulk of the present church is fourteenth century. King Richard and his family have a memorial window in the south aisle and his pennant is flown from the tower on significant dates

Go through the gate and walk straight across the field to a black metal gate. Turn right, down the path, to the road.

Middleham is twinned with Agincourt, scene of a great English victory over the French in October 1415. Henry V was outnumbered by a huge army of French knights in this set piece of the Hundred Years War (which lasted 116 years!) but the English archers won the day. When captured, archers had their bow-string fingers cut off by the French, and the remaining archers taunted the French with a certain two-fingered salute to show them that English firepower was not diminished.

Go straight over the housing estate road and walk along the lane to a stile and gate. Go into the field and walk ahead along the wall to the next boundary.

A few metres into the field is the site of St Alkelda's well, built into the wall on the left. The site of the well is hard to find today but is only a few metres from the public footpath. It is in very poor condition and is now just a hole in a dry stone wall, the water having been 'cut off ' when the new school and houses were built in 1988 and 1999. St Alkelda was a chaste Saxon princess who was killed by Vikings, reputedly in the viscinity of the holy well, which was subsequently believed to have healing virtues. Little else is known about her, and her very existence is doubted, especially when one realises that the Saxon word for 'holy well' is haelig-keld. Her feast day is celebrated on 28th March.

Go through the stile and turn right down the hill. In the bottom corner of the field turn left. Just before the corner of the field go through a narrow squeeze-stile on the right and turn left. Follow the wall along to a stile on the left in a section of wall. Go through the stile, turn right and follow the bottom of the field to a red gate that leads out into a large field.

The market town of Leyburn is clearly visible across the river valley. On the fourth Saturday of each month, wonderful locally grown and reared produce is sold at the farmers' market in the town square.

View over the Ure Valley, Wensleydale.

The path begins to swing around and down to the right towards the bottom left-hand corner. Go through the gate, walk up the bank and follow the bottom edge of the field along to another gate. Go through the gate and turn right to another gate, and then head out directly across the field, passing through a line of hawthorn trees on the way to a red gate. Turn left.

In late May, the landscape is white with hawthorn blossom. In Wensleydale it is easy to see why the hawthorn is the most common hedgerow shrub in the country.

Follow the track, with the bank on the left, to where the hawthorn hedge on the right ends, just before the ruined barn. Turn right and walk ahead towards the river keeping to the right-hand side of a line of trees. At the river, turn left over a farm bridge and through a gate. Continue ahead with the wooded riverbank on the right.

The name of the forget-me-not gained popularity during the Romantic movement of the early nineteenth century. The small blue-petalled flowers are common on open and disturbed ground, and the shape of the curved stalk is said to resemble that of a scorpion, hence its other name, 'scorpion grass'.

The bridge over the Ure, Wensley.

After a short distance the path cuts through the trees on the right and comes out beside the River Ure.

The river is home to many bird species, including kingfisher, merganser, heron, mallard, redshank, oystercatcher, black-headed gull and lapwing. Halcyon is a poetic name for the kingfisher, which is common along this stretch of the River Ure. In Greek mythology, the alkuon was a fabulous bird that calmed the stormy winter seas, and hence was a prelude to fine, if unseasonal, weather. These 'halcyon days', therefore, refer to a fortnight of fine weather during the winter solstice.

Follow the path as its sweeps round the bend with the river on the right and a sweeping line of hawthorn trees on the left. Follow the river all the way to the bridge, walking on the low flood defence banking. Take the path on the left up onto the road, and then turn right and return to the Three Horseshoes.

Bowes and Scargill Castles, and Mortham Tower

27.5 km/17 miles

Explorer OL31 *North Pennines –*
Teesdale and Weardale

Start from the George and Dragon in Boldron

Walk up to the telephone box and turn right. Keep straight ahead at the junction, and then walk up the drive – a public footpath – to West Hall just before the bend.

> *St George is the patron saint of chivalry and the guardian saint of England and Portugal. His origins are rather obscure. He may have been tortured and put to death by the Roman emperor Diocletian on 23rd April 303. The story of his fight with a dragon first appeared in Voragine's* Legenda Aurea, *(meaning Golden Legend) written in the thirteenth century. The Crusades gave great impetus to the cult.*

Walk straight past the house and through the gate. Turn right to a stile in the wall, and then walk diagonally across the next field to another stone stile. Walk across the next field, aiming for the left-hand side of the green painted barn. Walk around the barn and go through the gate in front of the house. Turn left up the lane to the gate.

> *This is West Roods Farm. A rood is a measure of land, equalling one quarter of an acre, or 40 square rods. A rod measured 16½ feet.*

Just before the gate turn right to a stile and then walk along the top

211

of the field to a lane. At the lane go straight ahead past the front of the house and through a gate. The path veers to the left through the small wood to another gate. Strike out straight up the field to a stile on the top wall, slightly to the right.

The path meets the A66 here, which runs along the line of the Roman road that linked Carlisle on the western side and York on the eastern side of England.

Do not climb the stile, but turn right and head down the field towards North Side Farm. In the bottom left-hand corner of the field, climb into the small plantation, walk through the saplings, and climb out the other side. Turn left to a gate and then walk across the field aiming for a stile to the left of the house.

The red clover that is grown for animal fodder tends to stand erect on grasslands and waysides, whilst the true native variety sprawls across the ground and has darker red flowers. The main difference between red and white clover is that the red has a leafy stem and the white has a leafless stem. Both are good sources of nectar for bees.

Cross directly over the lane and walk past the chicken coops to a wide metal gate. Go through the gate and straight across the field. Follow the path over the fences and walls past the front of the house to a stile in the wall. Cross the next two fields to a narrow gateway and turn left up the bridleway that runs beside the quarry workings. Follow the quarry boundary fence ahead and then right, and walk down to the access road.

This is Bowes Limestone quarry, from which aggregate, i.e. crushed up rock, is removed for road building.

Cross directly over the road through the gates and then over the stile into the trees on the right. Turn left up the bank and keep within the trees to follow the fence ahead and then right to another stile that leads to a track. Turn right.

The path through here is not clearly marked and signs imply that one should not even be on this side of the fence. However, the stiles imply otherwise. Alternatively, stay in the field and follow the fence to the gate, turn right and walk up the track.

Myre Keld Farm.

At the junction turn left down towards High Broats Farms. Just before the farm turn right, over a stile, and walk straight ahead across two fields towards the disused railway. Just before the railway, turn left and head towards a stile over an electric fence into the lane.

The name broats *is from the Old Norse meaning 'a fragment, or small piece of land'.*

Cross the lane and keep heading left towards a stile in the wall, now walking parallel to the railway embankment. The path now follows the base of the embankment all the way to Myre Keld Farm, crossing several fields on the way.

Myre Keld Farm is named after a 'muddy' myre 'spring' keld.

Go straight on along the line of wooden farm buildings, which are built on the line of the old railway. Climb the stile into the lane and head down towards the house. Just before the house, turn right through a gate. Walk down the side of the hedge and then left through the gap, back onto the footpath. Turn right and walk ahead and around the pond to a stile in the wall.

Many footpaths have been diverted from their traditional route by legal or other means. Despite landowners knowing that footpaths cross their land and are registered on a definitive map, many have re-routed paths so as not to disturb their privacy. In most cases the changes are slight in that they do not

213

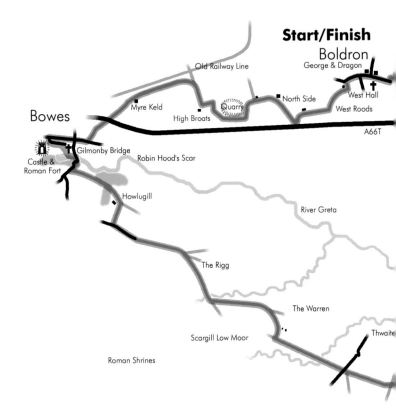

Start/Finish

Boldron

George & Dragon

Old Railway Line

North Side

West Hall

West Roods

Myre Keld

Quarry

High Broats

A66T

Bowes

Gilmonby Bridge

Robin Hood's Scar

Castle & Roman Fort

Howlugill

River Greta

The Rigg

The Warren

Thwaite

Scargill Low Moor

Roman Shrines

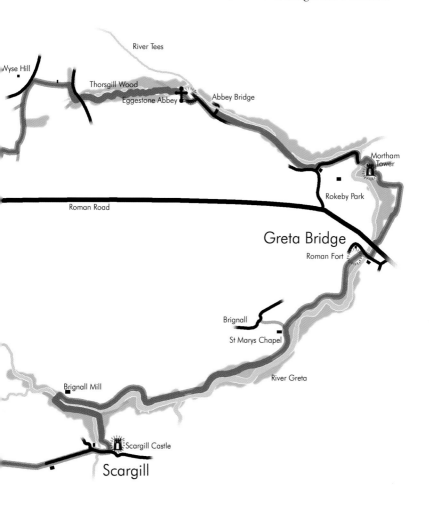

River Tees

Wyse Hill

Thorsgill Wood

Eggestone Abbey

Abbey Bridge

Mortham Tower

Roman Road

Rokeby Park

Greta Bridge

Roman Fort

Brignall

St Marys Chapel

River Greta

Brignall Mill

Scargill Castle

Scargill

veer too far from the original route. In other cases, the diversions are unacceptable and should be put right by responsible county council rights of way departments.

Cross directly over the field to a stile hidden beneath the trees. Follow the hedge line on the right, past a small farm building and keep on the same line all the way to a stile in the wall on the left where the fence ends. Walk through the undergrowth to another stile and then drop down the embankment to cross the main road.

Burdock is a common plant in such habitats. It is well-known for its 'sticky' buds that have small hooks, which were the inspiration for Velcro – the name being an amalgamation of 'velvet' and 'crochet hook'. The fruits would attach to passing livestock and become scattered in the surrounding countryside. The roots and young shoots are edible and it is an ingredient of the traditional northern drink, dandelion and burdock.

Take care in crossing. Once over the road walk up the banking just to the right as indicated by a sign. Walk up through the nettles to a stile, and then another stile in the wall. Walk over the narrow field to another wall, and then turn 45° to the left, down the field to a gate half way along the fence. Keep on this line through a gateway in the far wall, and then cross the last field to the far corner. Climb out onto the road and turn right into the village.

Bowes is the 'place where the river bends'. When John Leland visited in the time of Henry VIII, he mentioned that, 'Watling Street runs from Boroughbridge to Carlisle' and passes through Bowes, 'a dreadfully poverty-stricken roadside place'.

Walk all the way up the road through the village of Bowes to a back lane, which leads to the castle.

Bowes Castle stands within the site of the Roman fort of Lavatrae (meaning 'riverbed'), and both were built to guard the Stainmore Pass, a busy line of communication from Roman times to the present. It was started by Conan the Little, Earl of Richmond, and finished by Richard the Engineer, for Henry II between 1171 and 1187. It comprises a massive Norman keep, with a ditched platform. Bowes was more a garrison post than a residential castle for it was a solitary keep that stood without the protection of curtain walls. A rectangular ditch enclosure was its only outer defence. It was captured by local barons during the anarchy of 1322, when Thomas of Lancaster tried to usurp the ineffectual king, Edward II. The Roman fort was probably occupied during the second century, although little remains apart from earthworks and ditches. The stone was used in the building of the castle and church. Stone from the castle was later used in houses in the village.

Follow the lane round to the left behind the church.

The Church of St Giles was restored in 1865, but still contains a late-Norman door and the south porch of 1404. The Norman font stands on five thirteenth-century supports. Amazingly, in the north transept lies a stone slab marking the dedication of the building which can be dated back to 204–8AD, when the Romans had a fort here.

After a short distance go over the stile on the right into the field, aiming for the gateway in the far wall. Head down the next field to the centre of the bottom boundary. Climb the stile and walk down the steps to the banks of the River Greta and turn left to the road. Turn right over Gilmonby Bridge and walk up the lane to a footpath on the left.

The suffix '-by' on a place-name, as in Gilmonby and Rokeby, implies Scandinavian settlement in the ninth and tenth centuries.

Cross three fields towards a wood. Walk along the side of the wood and then head right to take a path through the trees, dropping down to cross a small stream. Head diagonally up across the next field to a track. Turn left for a short distance and then turn right up the hill towards the farm at Howlugill.

Back down at the river is a high cliff called Robin Hood's Scar. As most people now know, Robin Hood was a Yorkshireman who lived in and around the forest of Barnsdale near Barnsley. There are many place-names relating to this legendary outlaw, but whether he visited any of them is open to debate. There are tales that he visited Nottingham, but far more literary and historical evidence survives suggesting that he spent most of his time in Yorkshire. He is buried near Kirklees Abbey outside Huddersfield.

Walk up the left-hand side of the buildings and then turn left to a stile below a solitary tree. Go over the stile onto a lane. Follow it left and then right, all the way up the hill to the road. Turn left and follow it to where it ends. Go through the gate onto a green lane. Follow this to where it ends. Go through a gate and head out at 45° to the right onto The Rigg.

The paths over this area of heather and bilberry moorland are very hard to spot in clear weather, let alone in mist. Rigg is a Scandinavian word meaning 'ridge'. This moor is a breeding

The massive keep of Bowes Castle.

Scargill Low Moor.

ground for red grouse, and the number of shooting butts indicates where a lot of them will end up.

Walk ahead to the brow of the hill keeping the wall in sight down on the right. (In mist, simply follow the wall on the right all the way round to the footbridge.) Cross a path at right-angles and go straight on aiming for where the wall dips to cross a stream. Cross the footbridge and walk up the banking and through the wall. Keep ahead up the hill to a track.

This is now Scargill Low Moor. About a mile away, up to the right to the west of Spanham Farm, a series of Roman shrines were found on grassy platforms cut into the hillside and lined with dressed stone. They were dedicated by Roman centurians to the gods Silvanus and Vinotonus Silvanus.

Turn left and follow the track down the valley with the wall on the left. The path eventually swings round to the right to a metal gate – do not go through it but keep ahead following the wall around to the right, as it swings up the hill beside a field called The Warren. A small hut stands just over the wall in the corner of the next field.

The Warren was probably an area where rabbits were bred for food and fur.

On the crest of the hill take the gate on the left. Walk straight ahead over the rough open moor to a wall. Follow the wall round to the right. Keep beside the wall as it drops down and over a stream. Go over the stream and follow the wall round to the left. At the next wall turn right and walk ahead to the road.

This road leads left to the village of Thwaite, an Old Norse name meaning 'clearing', which is often suffixed to either a personal or geographic name, as in Garnathwaite up the road the other way.

Cross directly over the road and follow the bridleway ahead with the wall on the left. Keep beside this wall through a number of gates. When two gates are met side by side, go through the left-hand one and follow the track that becomes Moor Lane all the way to the road, passing through two red wooden gates on the way.

The small hamlet of Scargill is derived from 'the ravine' gill frequented by 'cormorants' skraki.

At the road turn right and follow it down and over the stream. Take the footpath on the left just over the bridge and walk ahead through the field keeping to the left-hand wall. Up to the right is Scargill Castle Farm.

All that remains of Scargill Castle are fragments of fifteenth-century masonry within a gatehouse, although it has been much altered and restored. The first reference to Scargill was in the Domesday Book of 1086, and by 1180 the lord of the manor was Warin de Scargill. Members of the family fought in the Crusades and the Anglo-Scottish wars, and the estates stayed with the family until the sixteenth century. The original castle included an ancient pele tower of three storeys and covered about two acres of ground. A short distance up the road are the remains of the chapel. Rumours abound that a subterranean passage leads from the castle to Egglestone Abbey. But this seems rather far fetched – it's a long way!

Go through the gate in the corner of the field to the left of the farm, and walk down the green terraced path that follows the stream down through the woods towards the River Greta. Just before the river, turn left to cross a wooden footbridge. Follow the River Greta upstream

Scargill Castle.

along the wooded banks to another footbridge on the right over the river.

The heron is the largest long-legged British wading bird. It generally breeds in trees in colonies, but spends the rest of its time in the solitary pursuit of fish. It is easily distinguished by its size, grey plumage and black eye stripe.

Turn right downstream and, after a very short distance, go up the stone steps on the left into the garden of the house. Walk ahead and go through the gap in the wall to the left of the horse paddock. Walk along the wooden fence and then drop down into the dip on the left. A marker post indicates where to turn left to the white gate and the drive of Brignall Mill. Turn right up the drive and walk to the top of the hill and over the cattlegrid.

Cattlegrids are commonly used to stop livestock from wandering where not wanted without passing traffic having to stop and open gates. Cows, sheep and pigs are have long been the predominant domesticated animals in England. After the Norman Conquest, the invaders dominated society, usurping Anglo-Saxons from their manors and estates. The English were relegated to looking after farm animals and the names of

The ruins of St Mary's Chapel near Brignall.

*livestock – cow, sheep and pig – have remained Anglo-Saxon. However, their new lords were those who ate the meat accounting for French/Norman origins of 'beef' (*beouf*), 'mutton' (*mouton*) and 'pork' (*porc*).*

Once in the field, turn right into the field along the top of the wood. After a few hundred yards the path goes through a gate back into the woods, and all the way down to the riverside. The path now follows the river all the way back to Greta Bridge.

Within these woods can be seen the very distinctive flower called lords-and-ladies. The flower is a small club-shaped pod surrounded by a pale green cowl. The bright red berries cluster on stout cylindrical spikes in the autumn. There are many other pretty flowers to be seen in these woods.

The path meanders along and up and down the steep banks, which are prone to subsidence and flooding. At one point in the rocky banks of the gorge is a large cave. New saplings have been planted in some of the low-lying meadows. Keep along the bank until eventually a stile leads out into a meadow, in the centre of which are the remains of an old chapel.

> *This is the old Church of St Mary that once served the deserted medieval village of Brignall. The 'new' Brignall – 'nook' halh of the followers of a man called Bryni – is half a mile to the west. The village has a new church, built in 1833–34 to replace this much older church on the banks of the River Greta, of which only the east wall stands.*

Walk through, or round, the graveyard to a sign beside an old barn. Turn right through the wall and walk up the hill to the top of the wood. The path now follows the top of the banking along the edge of large open fields. The path climbs a stile but stays out of the wood. Eventually, the path drops down through the field to the riverside. Go ahead through a gate and keep going ahead to the road.

> *On the left at this point are the earthwork remains of the Roman fort of Magnola. As the Romans advanced northwards they soon realised the strategic importance of the route over the Pennines, and that it would need guarding. This fort was built to guard the ford over the River Greta and was probably occupied during the second to fourth centuries. It was built to a typical rectangular plan and defended by a single bank and ditch. The entrance is in the centre of the south rampart and some stone is still visible.*

The Roman fort at Greta Bridge.

At the wall turn right over the bridge.

Greta Bridge was built in 1773, and has one large 80ft arch with a balustraded parapet. Across the road are the grand gates that once served Rokeby Park.

Cross Greta Bridge and take the footpath sign on the left, marked 'Meeting of the Waters' (the confluence of the rivers Greta and Tees) and 'Barnard Castle'. Walk straight across the field, with the river on the left, and through a gate that leads to the underpass beneath the main road. Follow the signs, taking the path to the right of the fence, and walk up the hill with the wood on the left. Follow the edge of the wood to a small, red wooden gate in the hedge, and then follow the line of a former hedgerow to a wall-less barn straight ahead.

Guinea fowl can be seen wandering around this farmland. This exotic poultry bird originates from Africa where it is also seen running around farms being used as a watchdog. Those with the entire feathered portion covered with small white dots are described as 'pearled'.

At the barn, turn left down the track to a stile by the gate. Follow the track down to the right towards the pond and then turn left round the buildings towards Mortham Tower.

The house that incorporates Mortham Tower is built around a courtyard with a south wall and gateway. The hall is in the north range, with the later medieval tower and an attached wing to the north west. The tower is square, with a modern flat roof behind a parapet and a north-east stair turret. It is a Grade I Listed building. The Rokeby family built Mortham Tower in the fourteenth century following the destruction of their former residence by Scots raiders in 1314. It was much altered and added to but by the eighteenth century it was used as a farm outbuilding until its restoration in 1939. The tower has interesting unglazed upright windows instead of battlements around the parapet.

By the gates of the house turn right down the drive and follow it as it swings around to the lane, crossing a cattle grid and the rocky River Greta.

Mortham Tower.

> *This is the Dairy Bridge, an old rustic stone structure, densely covered with ivy and very picturesque. The rock formations in this section of the river comprise large, almost cubic, slabs of limestone.*

Turn right at the lodge and follow this narrow road all the way to the next road junction, now with the River Tees on the right and Rokeby Park on the left.

> *Sir Thomas Robinson built Rokeby Hall in 1731, after his marriage to the daughter of the Earl of Carlisle. It is a fine example of a Palladian-style country house, containing a unique collection of eighteenth-century needle-painting pictures, many interesting pieces of period furniture and an unusual print room. Rokeby was the setting for a ballad of the same name by Sir Walter Scott, written in 1813. As an antidote to his Scottish ballads, Rokeby was set in the midst of the Civil War. He hoped sales would help raise funds to finance the building of his new home at Abbotsford. Rokeby means 'rocky farm'.*

Just before the junction, turn right through a gate onto the wooded banks of the River Tees.

The path is now following the Teesdale Way, marked by a sign of the dipper. This distinctive little white-breasted bird is a common sight along the Tees, and other fast flowing rivers and streams. It often nests under waterfalls and is remarkable for its method of walking into and under water in search of insect larvae and freshwater shrimps. It gets its name from its characteristic habit of bobbing up and down on stones in the river.

Follow the path along the fence to a series of steps that wind down towards the river's edge. Cross a small stream by stepping stones between two squat metal marker posts.

Large sycamore, beech, oak and lime trees tower above a lush floor covering of butterbur, rose bay willow herb and Himalayan balsam, an escapee from Victorian gardens that has since spread rapidly along riverbanks throughout the country. It was introduced from the Himalayas but is now widely naturalised along riverbanks and on damp waste ground. It has upright, reddish stems that carry leaves in whorls of three or opposite pairs. The pretty flowers are pink, but the most interesting – and unexpected – features of this plant are the exploding seedpods.

Go over the stile and continue along the wooded riverbank, as the path climbs up and down following the river gorge.

Almost from its source, the River Tees forms the boundary between Yorkshire on the south bank and County Durham to the north. In the 1960s, the Borough of Teesside was created, and later in 1974 the so-called 'county' of Cleveland formed. The new 'county' claimed land from both sides of the river and Teesside's identity as distinct from Durham and Yorkshire was finally recognised. More controversial was the removal of the south side of rural Teesdale from Yorkshire into Durham. However, in reality, these are just administrative areas. The true counties still exist within their traditional boundaries – south of the Tees is still Yorkshire!

Follow the river all the way to the Abbey Bridge.

Egglestone Abbey.

This spectacular single-arch span with castellated parapets was built in 1773. Despite being far inland, cormorants can be seen fishing in this section of the dark, peat-coloured water. The cormorant is the largest all-dark British sea bird. Although it normally breeds on cliffs and rocky islets around the coast, it can also occasionally be found on fresh water inland.

Climb up the steep bank beside the bridge and come out on the road. Turn left briefly, and then right towards the abbey.

The Premonstratensian Abbey at Egglestone was founded by Ralph de Malton c.1196. It is cruciform in plan but without aisles. Much of the nave and chancel survive. The east end of the cloisters was converted into a house after the Dissolution by Robert Strelley in 1548. It still stands with its mullioned windows and looks very much the Elizabethan manor house.

> *More recently the ruins were consolidated and tidied up by the Ministry of Works in the early twentieth century. 'Eggle's-ton' was the farmstead ton of a man called Ecgel.*

Turn up the lane before the abbey, and then take the footpath immediately after the car park on the right. Walk diagonally across the field to the far end of the wall on the left. Walk round the corner and down the hill to the footbridge.

> *This is Thorsgill Beck. The name is of Scandinavian origin – beck 'a stream', gill 'a ravine' and Thor the 'God of war', indicating that this area came under the jurisdiction of the Danelaw, the eastern half of England conquered by the Danes at the time of Alfred the Great.*

Cross the stream and turn left along the bank to a stile that leads into the wood. Follow the path through the dense undergrowth to a ford and then continue ahead now with the stream on the right.

> *The distinctive finely-toothed, lobed leaves of the common lady's mantle can be seen proliferating in these woods. It is a member of the rose family and has small yellowish-green flowers. It thrives in damp woodlands and meadows.*

Follow this path all the way through the wood to a stile, after which the path turns left up the banking to the road. Cross directly over the road and walk up into the trees to a fence. Turn right and walk down some stone steps to a bridge over a section of the old road.

> *This is Thorsgill Bridge. Much of the old road has become overgrown having been superseded by the new road, the B6277.*

Walk up the road to the gate. Just after the gate take the footpath down the track on the left towards a small barn.

> *Over to the right at this point it is possible to see the town of Barnard Castle and the castle standing guard over the River Tees.*

Keep straight ahead past the barn across the next two fields to the road. Just before the road turn left inside the field to a stile. Follow the heavily overgrown path down the hedge to another stile. Climb into the open field and walk ahead along the hawthorn hedge line.

Ash trees line this hedgerow. They can be identified by their narrow, paired leaves and winged fruit, which hang in bunches.

Keep ahead on this same line through another field gate and down to a stream. Cross the stream and go up the field to another gate. Keep ahead to another stile and then veer to the right across the field to go through a gateway. Follow the hedge to another gate and then walk out across the next field aiming for a barn in the distance. Go over a stile to the left of the gate and then turn right. Follow the ditch and fence all the way along, passing over several former hedge lines, to the small enclosure.

This whole area was once covered with narrow strip fields, although modern farmers have uprooted many hedgerows to make larger, more easily farmed fields.

Walk along the bottom of the fenced enclosure and then turn left. Just after the building on the right, turn right over a stile and follow the lane ahead and then left into the village.

This is Boldron, the 'clearing' rum *used for 'bulls'* boli.

At the road turn right, and walk the short distance ahead passing the Primitive Methodist chapel and Boldron church to the junction. The George and Dragon is just down on the right.